To Terri
Thanks for
THON 2003!

Thomas
Baldrick

MW00674375

A Million & One Ways to Celebrate a Child

By
Thomas Baldrick

Author of KIDS RULE! The Hopes and Dreams of 21st Century Children

www.baldrick.com

Published by Popular Demand Book Company, LTD
P.O. Box 16216
Philadelphia, PA 19114-6216

First edition.

Baldrick, Thomas
    A Million and One Ways to Celebrate a Child / Thomas Baldrick.–
    Philadelphia, PA: Popular Demand Book Company, LTD. 2003

    1. Parenting.   2. Inspiration.   3. Title.

Library of Congress Control Number: 2002096956

ISBN: 0-9708-121-1-6

SAN: 253-9225

To the 40 heroic passengers and crew members of
United Airlines Flight 93 on September 11, 2001:

Thank you for your immeasurable generosity.
You gave away everything you ever had, ever wanted,
and everything you ever loved.

While your souls rest in eternal peace, I honor your
eternal gifts left here on earth for the children of today,
tomorrow, and the tomorrows thereafter. Being the
extraordinary, everyday people you were, you have given
children timeless teachings on subjects such as bravery,
sacrifice, dignity, destiny, and patriotism.

May the hearts of your loved ones be warmed, knowing your
legacy will live and grow, as children learn all about the 9-11
tragedies. As I work closely with your families to preserve your
memory, please bless us with your guidance and keep us as
united in our efforts as you were in yours.

I celebrate you, the "Fab 40," the first soldiers to fight
terrorism on the homeland of 21st Century America.
Though unarmed and unprepared for battle over the skies
of my native Pennsylvania, you were unbreakable and
will forever remain undefeated.

Thank you for celebrating children and leading them
so powerfully by example.

Contents

Thomas Baldrick, "A Champion for Children."
Photo by Mark Garvin.

Celebrating Thomas Baldrick

When it comes to celebrating me, I remain a "work in progress." Often, I am one of the last people to go to my party. Such are the consequences of being much too hard on myself, and much too impatient to wait for help from the universe to make a difference with my life.

I urge children, young and old, to like themselves and love themselves enough to be the unique person they are, and to do what they love, despite what others think or say. I can preach that message with power and proof, having safely passed that critical point on my life's journey.

In my career, I've seen that *"Luck is where preparation meets opportunity."* I've been lucky enough to taste success often. Yet, to do so, I truly have worked harder than a one-legged guy in a butt-kicking contest.

Becoming an author has taken me on the wildest roller coaster ride of my life. It may also be the greatest gift I've ever given to myself. The thrill (and challenge) of writing this book has matched or even surpassed the pinnacle of my first book, *KIDS RULE! The Hopes and Dreams of 21st Century Children*.

I cherish the higher platform that being an author has given me. Work as a heartfelt public speaker, a partner to various charities, and an author who visits schools, provides thrills and opportunities I love deeply.

As a television journalist, I've also been blessed with the excitement and experiences of covering major stories and events, meeting many VIP's, even winning six Emmy Awards. For more information, please log on to my website at www.baldrick.com.

While reading this section tells you something about my background, reading this book will tell you who I am.

Ready Or Not, Here I Come!

I'll admit, using the line from the child's game of Hide n' Seek is an unusual way to introduce a book. I don't know if it's ever been done before. But, that's no reason not to do it. The idea came wrapped so neatly in the form of a gift, I just had to take the chance.

The many distractions of my everyday life in Philadelphia were getting the best of me as a writer. I was feeling the need to hide for a few days from everyone and everything. Mother Nature held a cure for a classic case of writer's block like mine. It was found in a peaceful, secluded setting, where I could open my heart, stretch my mind, and work easily with passion.

My friend, Sharla Feldscher, and her husband Barry, were kind enough to offer me use of their empty beach house in Ventnor City, NJ (south of Atlantic City). So, in order to coincide with a scheduled author visit at a nearby school, I excitedly headed to their great place on the shoreline of the bay.

Fall's crispness was in the air, having chased away the crowds of summer tourists. Mother Nature must be a big fan of writers. For most of my five-day visit, she prevented outside distractions by crying tears of joy for me from her place high up in the sky. More importantly, she used the smell of her salt-water seas to hold my writer's block at bay.

I had been seeking only a "writer's getaway." Instead, I got upgraded to "a romantic getaway," just my laptop computer and me. My fingers were flowing freely on the keyboard, as CD's soothed us with the sounds of Secret Garden's, "Songs from a Secret Garden," and my friend Dean Arvidson's, "Heart Lake."

Thomas Baldrick interviewing Britney Spears for "Entertainment Tonight."

Sharing a laugh with Tom Cavanagh, star of NBC-TV's "Ed."

All this, and a spectacular full window view of the water—it was a sheer LoveFest. (Could you tell I am a Pisces?)

The right environment is a major advantage for me as a writer. It works instantly. Therefore, while the way the idea for this book's introduction came to me might seem unusual to you, it was really quite ordinary to me. I do hear voices, and I know it is easier to receive their loving guidance when I have the support of silence.

So, it was no surprise when I heard the words, *Ready or not, here I come,* as I opened the door to the beach house. Immediately, I jotted them down and placed the note on the dining room table next to my computer. After only a few hours of their hiding and me not seeking, I was ready to know why those words came to me, and how I would use them.

As I was finishing writing another section of this book, it dawned on me that in the game of Hide n' Seek, when you are "it," your mission is to seek and find the other players. In essence, this is *exactly* what I'm doing in my mission as an author.

I am seeking to find charities, schools, corporations, organizations, associations, events, and individuals with an interest in joining me to make the world a better place, especially for children. I am seeking to find people who would enjoy reading this book, whether they are male or female, black or white, young kids or young-at-heart grownups like me.

With this book, I am also seeking to inspire others to create bigger, better and more frequent celebrations of children. One doesn't have to look far to find a child in need of being celebrated. They most definitely are not in hiding anywhere.

If you look up "celebrate" in various dictionaries, the consensus you'll find is that it means *to praise or publicly honor something or someone special.* The description works well for this book, but only to a certain extent. You should know I'm also using the word "celebrate" as an umbrella term to cover an array of ways for sharing love with a child.

Here, you will read ideas for how to appreciate a child, how to help a child, teach a child, have fun with a child, and respect a child. Some of these ideas you may already remember. Others you may find will be good or helpful for you to *start* remembering.

But this is so much more than a book of lists. The pages are filled with inspiring and heartwarming stories about unique ways grownups are celebrating children. In addition, there are touching tales of children who are shining little stars, quite worthy of celebration.

After I finished writing my first book, *KIDS RULE! The Hopes and Dreams of 21st Century Children*, but before its release, I was led to get started on this book, selecting it from my list of ideas as an author. The writing has come in a handful of waves over the course of roughly a year and a half. During this time, I feel I have grown tremendously from experiences related to *KIDS RULE!*

As you could probably tell by reading this book's dedication, the 9-11 tragedies have also affected me deeply. Beginning moments after the first tower of the World Trade Center was hit, I worked nearly a month straight for ABC News, covering the story as a television journalist in New York, and later from Shanksville, PA. Like many, I was forever changed by those events. Hopefully, I am a better person for it, not to mention a more powerful writer.

More and more, I find myself believing that reality is a meaningless term. There is only perception. If ten of us were to see the same thing, we could likely have ten different accounts as to what happened. Who's to say which person's perception is correct, and therefore reality?

I share this insight because my initial perception in doing this book was that it would be difficult to come up with A Million & One ways to celebrate a child. My reality was I couldn't have been more wrong. Ready or not, the ideas came. Throughout the creative process in writing this book, I have never strayed far from a pen and paper, scribbling notes in the shower, at the gym, while driving, eating, and trying to fall asleep!

The stories in this book are true examples of ways that celebrate a child. Stories continue to come at me with such force and frequency, that I am already considering a sequel to this book as my next published work.

Sadly enough, *Ready or not, here I come,* is also a fitting theme for me personally. It is the way I have viewed my place in life many times in the past few years. "Ready" is not a word that comes to mind when I am totally open and genuine with others, showing who I am, what I feel, or what wisdom I've been given to share. I'm not sure whether it's more a case of the world not being ready for me, or me not being ready for the world. Nonetheless, I keep on saying, "Here I come!"

In the fall of 1998, more than fifteen years into the successful television career I had dreamed of since childhood, I conceded to needing something more in my life. The phrase I coined to describe my decision was, *"It got far too dangerous, for me to continue to play it safe."*

Through plenty of pain and hard work, I've developed a high level of self-awareness. It has benefited me greatly in dealing with children. It also enabled me to realize that even though I don't like it, my life flows best when I *let* things happen, rather than relying solely on my ability to *make* things happen. To do this, I need the courage to trust that if I *"Leap first, the rope shall appear."* Once in a while, (or at the very least once) it might be fun to know where my leaps of faith are leading me!

My life as an author, inspirational speaker, and deeply spiritual, single man who loves kids, is fulfilling and rewarding. Yet, it doesn't mean I'm free from feeling my terror. Quite the opposite is true. Coming so much from my heart in what I say and what I write, I feel like I'm constantly facing rejection. A steady but necessary diet of speeches, school appearances, and media interviews only adds to my feeling vulnerable.

I've invested so much time, effort and money into my mission that the world seems out of balance. My social life suffers. My love life does, too. Every day, this work feels as though I'm walking across rocks on water. I have no stability, no place to rest, and no idea what step is coming next. Oh yeah, there's also the constant fear of slipping and falling.

Having said all that, I know I am *exactly* where I'm meant to be, doing exactly what I'm meant to be doing. I wouldn't trade my path in life for anything. It helps to know I couldn't trade it, even if I tried. It is the hero's journey, and I am answering my soul's deepest longings. Along the way, I clearly see the signs and the amazing people who are here to help me. However, there are no u-turns or off-ramps in this line of work.

My burning desire is to grow and make a difference. I hope to experience as much as I can, and to touch as many souls as I can. Then, when I'm called home, and it's time for me to leave, hopefully in some small or big way, I'll have left this world a better place simply because I was here.

Whether you feel it was hidden, or whether you feel it "jumped out at you," this book is now in your hands. Either you found it, or the book found you. There are no accidents or co-incidences in life. There are only opportunities and experiences to be had. Of all the books ever written, the countless published works you could choose to read or ignore, realize that this book, in this moment, has gotten your attention.

It is likely these pages contain some piece of information your heart has been seeking. Perhaps, there is a cause, person, or something else inside this book seeking *your* attention.

All of us have childhood hurts we carry everywhere. Some of us try to hide them beyond the reach of our feelings. Others face them, and deal with them as best they can. We all have a child alive inside us. He or she is a little one, forever seeking to get his or her needs met. Whatever your reasons are for having this book, I thank you and honor you for being here now. I wish you the best and hope you move forward on your hero's or heroine's journey.

You may find this is a great book to leave on the coffee table, or somewhere else in your frequent line of vision. Having easy access to it will come in handy at times.

If you're feeling happy, and want to be inspired by the good-ness in the world, there are stories in this book to put a smile on your face, and in your heart. If you happen to find yourself the guest of honor at your own impromptu pity party, there are also stories in this book to bring out the tears you may need to release.

Marking certain pages may serve as helpful reminders if you have a child in your life. Perhaps, they will even provide the spark for your own creative ideas for celebrating a child.

Regardless of how you use this book, I sincerely hope you receive some rewards by reading *A Million & One Ways to Celebrate a Child.*

Last Time, First Time

When was the last time, you did something for the first time with a child? Perhaps, you can remember this question as you read this book and take in ideas for ways to celebrate a child.

See a child as a little person, not a possession.

Get a child to understand you care enough to sometimes say "no."

Say you'll answer a question later if it's best to think about your response.

Run a child in a shopping cart safely down the aisle.

Run up steps and jump around like in the movie "Rocky."

Savor a child's little smile.

Appreciate a child's little feet.

Appreciate a child's little hands.

Sing with a child.

Talk with a child, not at them or to them.

Build a tree house with a child.

Take a child out for afternoon teatime.

Give a child your undivided attention.

Ask a child to vent frustrations.

Do volunteer work with a child.

Wash your car together.

Give a child a massage.

Let a child give you a massage.

Diamonds Are A Child's Best Friend

Five-year old Colby Hoch said words to his mommy that no parent should ever hear. He asked, "If I die, how am I going to talk to you?" Little Colby was speaking with his mommy from a place of sadness and curiosity more so than fear. He knew he would be leaving her and his daddy before they ever watched him go to his first day of school, before he ever attended a prom, landed a job, or got married and had a child of his own. Being in the hospital as much as he was, Colby knew his fate. After all, he had watched many of his sick little friends die.

A few days after the ultimate question, Judy held Colby in her arms as he passed away. For at least another hour, she sat in the hospital room and held on for dear life to her first-born child, her precious baby boy. But Colby had gone; leaving his cancer-riddled little body behind. Six years later, Judy Hoch cannot, will not, let go.

Painstaking moments like this happen every single day. They are dying proof we still can't boast of how we've beaten childhood cancer. But, one weekend a year, thanks to an amazing event called THON™, we **can** say, "We beat the living *'you know what'* out of it!"

This is a tribute to *the largest student-run philanthropy in the world*. It is a true celebration of college kids who major in helping kids with cancer. THON™ is the trademarked (and much needed shorter) name for the Penn State Interfraternity Council/Panhellenic Dance Marathon. The slogan for everything they do, and everything they say, is "For the Kids."

Love, sharing, sacrifice, and self-abuse are the cornerstones of the weekend-long event held on campus in the recreation hall. The bleachers are literally packed with supporters. On the floor below, about 700 student gladiators battle themselves, not each other, in a *48-Hour, No-Sitting, No-Sleeping, No-Kidding* test of

Colby Hoch with his special THON™ friend, Brian.

endurance. The purpose is to raise money and hope for families dealing with childhood cancer. Lee R. Kimball, II, THON™ 2003 Overall Chairperson admits, "When you realize thousands of people mark this event on their calendars as something special like Christmas or birthdays, it gets really overwhelming."

For more than 30 years standing, THON™ weekend in February marks the happiest time of the year in the Central Pennsylvania college town known as "Happy Valley." "We think it's pretty special," says Jayme Rubright, Overall Chairperson for the 2002 event and a special young woman in her own right. "Everybody has their own causes. We're just doing our thing here in Happy Valley, one small corner of the world."

Alas, there is good reason to thank rowdy college kids (and I'm not saying this because I was one). It was because of them that back in 1973, the Interfraternity Council needed to do damage control for its image. An event was created at Penn State in which 39 couples set out to dance in a 30-hour competition to benefit the Pennsylvania Association for Retarded Children. Seventeen couples finished, and nearly $1,700 was raised for the charity. In each of the next two years, more than $10,000 was raised for the American Heart Association and the Easter Seals respectively.

In 1977, the competition between dance couples was replaced by a common goal of surviving 48 straight hours of standing. Another big change was that a little known charity called "The Four Diamonds Fund," became the event's beneficiary. Since then, it has become common knowledge around Penn State that *"Diamonds are a Child's Best Friend."*

The Four Diamonds story is truly a gem. The four memorable words—courage, wisdom, honesty, and strength—were written in 1972 by Christopher R. Millard, a fourteen-year old in the final year of his life. His essay entitled, "The Four Diamonds," was based on the four qualities he believed were essential in fighting cancer.

Though not quite as synonymous with Penn State as the name Paterno, the Millard name has become something of an institution. It didn't come from donating so much money that the university named a library after them. It didn't happen because

❖ COURAGE

❖ WISDOM ❖ HONESTY

❖ STRENGTH

26 members of their family have attended the university. The Millards became heroes simply because they did something positive to keep Christopher's name alive.

Soon after their son's death, Charles and Irma Millard established "The Four Diamonds Fund" with the Penn State Milton S. Hershey Medical Center. Sara Schimmer, coordinator of The Four Diamonds Fund, says, "Our core service is to provide care and take care of any expense that insurance will not cover. We cover car payments, utility bills, meal tickets, phone cards, gas vouchers to get back and forth between home and the hospital, even helping families when a parent is forced to take a leave from work due to their child's illness. We also have a pediatric staff, and various clinical, educational, and research programs supported through the fund." I told you it was a gem.

The Hoch's became a Four Diamonds family in 1994 after two-year old Colby's illness, originally diagnosed as pneumonia, turned out to be a very aggressive form of cancer, Stage 4 Neuroblastoma. Little Colby had a tumor in his adrenal glands. He had a bone marrow transplant because cancer was found there, too. It was in his spine, his little hips, his little legs—pretty much everywhere.

While Colby received the finest medical treatment for his rare disease, his father Len, and mother Judy, prefer to speak of an even more comprehensive form of treatment. Judy Hoch says, "The Four Diamonds Fund made Hershey the only medical facility we saw that treats the whole soul. It doesn't just treat the patient. All of the souls in our family were cared for, including Colby's."

Exceptional care and treatment were the reasons why in 1978, Jimmy Cefalo, the All-American wide receiver from Penn State's football team, made a pact with the Penn State Milton S. Hershey Medical Center that THON™ would benefit The Four Diamonds Fund as long as the monies would be used to fight pediatric cancer. (The nation had recently seen cancer beat Penn State. You might have heard the story of Penn State's star running back, John Cappelletti, the 1973 Heisman Trophy winner who lost his little brother Joey in a public battle with leukemia.)

THON™ has contributed roughly *25 million dollars* to The Four Diamonds Fund, and accounts for 85% of its total revenue. More than 2,000 families have been helped since the fund was founded. Each year, it supports 80 to 90 new families of child patients diagnosed with cancer.

How many charities do you know that are willing to rely on a bunch of college kids, a group and age bracket generally considered unreliable? "We prefer to look at it as a positive thing instead of having one large donor," laughs Sara Schimmer. "I think it just speaks volumes about Penn State students. The absolute truth is I've never met a more dedicated group of people in my life. They work very hard and care deeply about what they do. I often hear students say, 'Oh, I didn't get a lot of sleep this weekend or my school work can wait.' They really understand what is truly important to them and THON™ is such a major commitment."

Money is not the only way to measure the value and success of THON™. Every Penn State student organization adopts a Four Diamonds family. They remain in contact all year long, forming relationships that are priceless indeed. Lauren Ziatyk of the Gamma Phi Beta Sorority says, "Getting to see the kids and being able to put a face to this cause makes it so much better. We can see that our kids benefit directly from this event. It makes it so much stronger and so much more heartfelt. We care about the families as much as we care about ourselves."

Penn State's Rec Hall is filled with love during THON™.

Everything at THON™ is done "For the Kids."

Thank you THON™!

Here is a look at how the fundraising efforts of the event have grown over the years.

1977: $28,685.00

1982: $95,000.00

1985: $226,000.00

1990: $671,572.00

1992: $1,141,145.00 (reached $ 1 million for first time)

1998: $2,001,831.51 (reached $ 2 million for first time)

2000: $3,076,983.97 (reached $ 3 million for first time)

? - $ 5 million + ????

Lauren's sorority and the Kappa Alpha Fraternity proved how strong the bond between the students and their adopted family can get when they tested all of their members to find a match for a 10-year old boy with cancer who desperately needed a bone marrow transplant. A T-shirt I saw at THON™ said it all, *"The Stars of Today . . . helping the stars of tomorrow to shine brighter."*

As an institution of higher learning, the administration and faculty at Penn State are very understanding when it comes to THON™. They never lose sight of the big picture, even though they do lose sight of students in the classroom from time to time because the charity comes first. Former Penn State University President, Bryce Jordan, may have summed up THON™ best when he said, "It is an act of pure unselfishness."

Bob and Dorothy Cavaluchi of Silver Spring, MD agree. Their daughter, Christa, was involved with THON™ during all four of her years at Penn State. "This event is everything that's right about today's kids," says Bob. There's thousands of them needed to pull it off every year. And none of them *have* to do it."

Just because something is hard work doesn't mean it shouldn't be done, believes Jayme Rubright, who chaired THON™ 2002. "I don't regret a single minute of it. It was the best job I ever had and I didn't even get paid! Yes, it did take up all of my time. Many give up their free time, but we are constantly given something back. I never thought twice about THON™ being a sacrifice." (Jayme graduated in May 2002 with a degree in English and Secondary Education. She now works for The Four Diamonds Fund, and since she is so nice, I'll round off her final grade point average to a 3.8.)

"It's a full-time job," admits Jayme's successor, Lee R. Kimball, II. The Spanish and Business major with a 3.4 grade point average makes it sound simple when he says, "If you have to write a paper at three o'clock in the morning because you've been working all night on THON™, you just do it."

There is no last-minute cramming for THON™. All 2,880 minutes are planned for and scripted. Lee and 2,500 of his fellow students work year-round for THON™ weekend. Acting like America's youngest CEO, he has 14 student committees working under him, each headed by a chairperson. Every chair has 20 captains under their supervision. The captains then interview and select another 30 volunteers to work with them.

More than 250 student organizations are registered to raise funds for THON™. They work on 20-30 annual events including a family carnival, auctions, a 5-K run/walk, and a 3-on-3 basketball tournament. "Canning to beat cancer" is one of the coolest and most successful fundraising efforts according to the students. They go door to door and stand at traffic intersections in all kinds of weather, soliciting donations "For the Kids." (It's not only the collecting that is time consuming. You try counting thousands and thousands and thousands of pennies, nickels, dimes, quarters and various dollar bills!)

The more money an organization raises, the more dancers it gets to have on the floor for THON™. Usually, the minimum amount required is around $750. The organizations then vote for the members who get to dance. Many use this as an incentive. Jayme Rubright says, "It is a reward and an honor, and choosing who gets to do it gets pretty intense."

So you see, it all makes perfect sense to these college students. Punishment of a physical, mental, and emotional nature is not a deterrent when it comes to THON™. It is the goal, a source of pride, a badge of courage and a symbol of success.

You really must be at THON™ to believe it. I will do my best to set a scene for you, but if I don't do a great job, please don't condemn me as a writer. Some things in life are hard to explain. In case you won't take my word for it, here's what other more experienced Thonners had to say when asked to describe the event:

> *"That is my least favorite question. I still don't have a sufficient answer."*
>
> —JAYME RUBRIGHT, *THON™ 2002 Overall Chairperson*

> *"Whew! I don't know how to describe it. I can only say THON™ is my favorite thing on earth. It just amazes me."*
>
> —JEANETTE SCHREIBER, *Family Relations Captain*

> *"It is hands down what I am most proud of in life."*
>
> —JENNY MCCARTHY, *dancer*

> *"It honestly didn't sound real to me. Words can only do so much until you're actually there."*
>
> —SARA SCHIMMER, *The Four Diamonds Fund Coordinator*

> *(Laughter)*
>
> —LEE R. KIMBALL, II, *THON™ 2003 Overall Chairperson*

> *"It's home. It's just home. There is no other way to put it."*
>
> —JUDY HOCH, *mother of Colby, a Four Diamonds Child*

In attending THON™, one can feel the excitement even before entering Rec Hall. Groups of students loudly enter the building carrying hopes and good intentions, along with all kinds of personal favorite belongings for the weekend of indoor camping.

Once inside, people in the stands will watch little kids and college kids running around on the floor, seemingly having the time of their young lives. Parents allow their kids to wander off in the crowd with their new babysitters and buddies. Sometimes, they don't even know the student's name. At THON™, every child with cancer and every one of their healthy siblings are treated the same. Every little boy is a king. Every little girl is a queen.

Beach balls and balloons are merrily kept airborne, batted around from person to person through the arena. On the floor is such a heavily armed group of kids, even a newcomer can't help but notice that water pistols are one of the preferred weapons of choice in this battle against childhood cancer.

Don't get the impression for one minute that THON™ is 48 hours of fun and games. It most definitely is not. People take turns in feeling their physical and emotional pain from the effects of exhaustion.

Though most sleep-deprived dancers want to quit at one point or another during THON™, the reality is only a very small percentage actually do. Much of the credit for this goes to the students called "moralers." Keeping morale high is a must.

Roughly 850 official moralers work in shifts to nurture the dancers and keep them going. They bring gifts, fetch food and drinks, offer hugs and helping hands, as well as inspiration and encouragement. When the time comes for every dancer to face the demons in their darkest moments, it is the moralers who keep them from crumbling, while reminding them of the importance of making it for 48 straight hours.

Volunteer student trainers are equally valuable lifelines. They set up a M*A*S*H type area just off the dance floor where first aid and massages are available. Offering tubs of ice water and taped bandages, they are the new best friends of many feet that are painfully sore and swollen from standing.

Comfort and love are offered everywhere you turn at THON™, despite the fact there is just no way for a person to be comfortable standing for 48-hours straight. Even the dance floor is lined with tables that are helpful for storing food, drink, and various forms of activities. More importantly, the tables are mandatory for holding up every dancer at various times of trouble throughout the weekend.

Music plays a big part in maintaining the energy of everyone at THON™.

Though the event is called a dance marathon, and the participants are known as dancers, the only real dancing occurs during the line dance.

Every year, one student hosts a weekend at their family's home, where a large group of THON™ captains gather to write the lyrics for the line dance (and to get a couple of home-cooked meals). The song traditionally documents the pop culture events making news since the previous THON™. The line dance is taught to the dancers on Friday night, and then performed more than 40 times to keep them energized and awake. They mix up the times in using the song so that it can't be used to gauge the passing of hours. Regardless of when the line dance is done, it always serves as a powerful way to unify and ignite everyone in attendance.

To this day, it gives me chills when I recall what it felt like to hear more than a thousand voices merged into one while singing the words from a THON™ line dance. Here is one portion:

"We will get there ...
>
> *For - the - Kids!*
>
> *Dance, with all your heart,*
> *Love, with all your heart,*
> *THON, with all your heart,*
>
> *For - the - Kids!"*

A number of live bands do a nice job in performing on stage at THON™. However, even the best ones are no real match for Disc Jockey Larry Moore. He has worked on THON™ for nearly thirty consecutive years, which is longer than most of the current Penn State students have been alive. "We're kind of the hub of the wheel. We make the whole thing spin," explains Larry.

Legendary Larry Moore began as a student dancer in 1977. More Moores, his sons Alex and Steve, and his joyful wife Jodi, now join him every year. "Our first date was teaching people in wheelchairs to disco dance as couples. Our second date was as

The line dance energizes and unifies everyone at THON™.

Larry Moore showing why he's been a part of THON™ since 1977.

Special Olympics coaches," says Larry. (Do you think this husband
and wife knows how to celebrate a child?)

In addition to his lending support year round, THON™ actually turns out to be a 67-hour work weekend for Larry and his
team. It most definitely justifies the pair of one-hour power naps
he takes in the Rec Hall squash courts. Larry is the main man at
the microphone who must be on his toes as well as his feet. "It
doesn't matter what happens," he laughs. "If the 'what if?' happens,
we have to respond." Larry says he will roll with THON™ "until
the students tell me to go away."

Larry Moore is one of the many stories of how THON™ celebrates a child. Jeanette Schreiber is another. In January 1999,
Jeanette was a 16-year old high school junior when she was diagnosed with Acute Promyleocitic Leukemia. "It was pretty much
out of the blue," she said. "I didn't even really know what
leukemia was. Cancer has been through many of my family members. It's just been everywhere. My mom actually had cancer insurance, but expected to use it for her or my dad, never me."

Jeanette said her life was turned upside down. She told her
friends and teachers about the disease, but otherwise it remained
surreal for days. "Pretty soon, I got to a place and said, 'Let's deal
with this thing. Let's get rid of it.' I was in remission by March, and
finished active treatment by May. I was pretty lucky."

During her senior year of high school, Jeanette learned about
THON™ from a Four Diamonds social worker. Jeanette got a taste
of the event from students at a satellite campus of Penn State. She
then decided to follow some friends to the main campus for her
college education where she instantly became involved in
THON™. Jeanette said, "I couldn't wait to be a part of it. I didn't
even question getting involved."

And so, a tumultuous turn of events meant the person catered
to in the past was suddenly doing the catering. As a Family Relations
Committee Captain, Jeanette is the contact for new families. She
points out, "I never liked saying, 'Hi. I'm Jeanette. I'm a former Four
Diamonds child.' I wanted people to know me and like me for me.
For a while, I didn't let people know what was going on with me."

A turning point for Jeanette came when she was asked to speak during Family Hour at THON™. It is the extremely emotional conclusion to THON™, featuring touching talks, stories, and updates from children and family members of The Four Diamonds Fund.

Jeanette agreed to what amounted to her "coming out party." It is gripping speeches from the heart like hers that make Family Hour at THON™ like reaching the top of a mountain climb. The speech also gave Jeanette a new view of her own path. "I can bring others away from the pain knowing there is someone they can talk to who is like them," she says. "It gives them power to get through a tough situation. That's one of the great things about THON™. It is very therapeutic to be around others who know what you're going through and to feel understood. It is such a big part of healing."

Jeanette Schreiber is switching her major to Human Development and Family Studies because it will allow her to do child life work. Such a goal is cause for another celebration of THON™. "I got involved because I want to give back. I've been given something, new life, but all of the other students are indirectly affected. They just do it because they're great people," Jeanette says. "College kids get a bad rap about drinking and being rowdy. THON™ makes people see so much good in college kids. To know that there are students giving so much of themselves for people like me, is just too powerful for words."

I was blessed to have THON™ touch my life when I was encouraged to help with the event by Stacy Sockel, a Penn State grad working as a manager for Barnes & Noble. Arrangements were made for me to sign copies of my book, *KIDS RULE! The Hopes and Dreams of 21st Century Children* at THON™. As always, when I work with a charity I donate proceeds from book sales to the cause.

Penn State never really had me as a football fan. Season after season, the Nittany Lions team always had my alma mater, the Temple University Owls for lunch. Quickly, the soreness of the subject was forgiven and forgotten. The more conversations I had with students, the more I couldn't wait to experience my first THON™.

Shortly before the event, I had a revelation. I decided if the students could stand without sleep for 48 hours to support children with cancer, then by golly, I could too. Despite the fact I had graduated from college roughly 20 years earlier, I was convinced my strong desire to make a difference in the life of a child, and a strong and physically fit body, would enable me to complete a 48-hour book signing. Besides, I was already well-accustomed to getting little rest.

Finding someone to share my self-confidence was as difficult as getting someone to endure the 48 straight hours with me. I couldn't convince a single person (Penn State grads included) to make the three and a half-hour drive to spend part of the time with me. Ignorance was bliss. Had I known what kind of a solo mission I was undergoing, I may never have followed through.

Baldrick is the name of a famous TV character in a popular British TV show, "Blackadder." Baldrick always has "a cunning plan" that never fails to get him in trouble. Hence, I should have known better when it came to THON. I developed my own cunning plan to survive 48 straight hours on my feet. Custer had a plan, too.

The day before THON™ began like any other Thursday morning as I woke at 6:00 A.M. My plan called for a drastic change on the back end of the day. I had decided it was best for me to stay up much later than my usual bedtime around midnight. It took a real effort, but I worked and walked around like a zombie until roughly 4:00 A.M.

I was out cold the moment my head hit the pillow, and fully expected to remain that way until noon. At that time, I would rise, shower, dress and head off to THON™ on Friday afternoon feeling totally refreshed, and ready for the long haul.

A funny thing happened on the way to the perfect execution of my cunning plan. My "body clock" obviously never got the memo about the change in schedule. As a result, it knew no better than to wake me as it regularly does at 6:00 a.m. Ugh.

It was a backfiring to be remembered. I awoke in a fog, but could not fall back to sleep. To work off my fatigue and frustration, I went to the gym, knowing exercise always makes my body feel great. Once again it worked, albeit temporarily. Roughly halfway into the trek to Penn State, I began to feel drowsy. This was not a good omen or confidence builder for a safe Friday afternoon drive, not to mention my ability to stay awake and on my feet until Sunday night.

Emergency measures were put into place. I blasted music. I pulled over at rest stops for double shots of splashing water on my face and buying jolts of Mountain Dew. At times, I rolled the windows down to scream and to usher in the cold air of winter as I cruised down the highway.

Somehow, other unwanted things blew into the front seat. I was headed into the wind all right, with doubt, fear, anger, and shame making a long ride even longer. These stowaways made sure I knew I would not make it through THON™. Heck, I didn't even believe I would make it *to* THON™. My morning fog had lifted enough to see that much was clear.

Failure was not apparent. It was imminent. Already, I couldn't live with myself knowing I was quitting on college kids who embraced me, and many little kids with cancer. I couldn't tell which disappointment hurt more. The feelings would likely get worse, with no easy fix in sight for this new fraud I found in my mirror.

With about an hour's drive still to go, I prepared to surrender to my fatigue. I reached for my cell phone, and dialed the THON™ office. Frozen by fear, I could not bring myself to hit the send button. Creating a lie as a lame excuse was not my style and therefore not an option. So, I did what any outraged child would do. I threw an impromptu tempter tantrum, pounding the steering wheel of "Jane Honda," the new, green Honda CR-V I got in time for THON to make good use of the cargo space for hauling books.

I decided that if I was going to lose the fight it was going to have to be by knockout. Collapsing at THON™ would be humiliating, but a far more dignified form of defeat than quitting. There was simply no way I was going to throw in the towel with my pride wrapped neatly inside.

I arrived on campus as the night prepared its takeover from late afternoon. It was the best I felt all day. I easily made my more than a handful of long walks carrying 45-pound boxes of books into Rec Hall. I was given a table on the concourse level to do my signings. Quickly, I realized how much carrying the extra boxes had been worth the effort. It wasn't because book sales were so brisk, but rather the pleasant surprise of learning I had given myself something to lean on in those moments when my legs grew weary. Yippee!

I spent the first few hours making a number of new friends and acting like a sponge in soaking up knowledge about THON™. There was absolutely no doubt electricity was in the air. My only concern was how I would ward off my inevitable personal power outage.

In the wee hours that first night, I spent time down on the floor with the dancers. Other times, I walked laps around the concourse level, doing whatever might help me to stay awake. There were many occasions when I didn't even know what I was doing.

I will honestly admit that at times I got lost in my own woes. I'm not proud to say I forgot what I'd said earlier to my friends about, "Whatever pain I go through for 48 hours is nothing compared to what the little ones with cancer go through every day." Hearing that every dancer goes through similar moments is one of the many lessons I learned at THON™.

When your body is teetering on the brink of exhaustion, many strange things can happen. The experience made me aware of so many little things that I actually felt foolish having taken for granted my entire life. This is great information to share with others, especially a child.

A heightening of the senses was a big surprise to me. I could feel individual parts of my body and pain like never before. I recognized what food and drink made my body feel good, and what made it feel worse. Things such as going to the bathroom, shaving, and washing my face offered much higher forms of relief than ever before. I also never embraced the light of day like I did during the mornings of THON™ weekend. It is so wild to feel the effect that daylight can have on your energy level and your spirit.

With all due respect to the previous forms of enlightenment, it makes me sad to know it took sheer exhaustion to make me realize just how much each of us can make a difference with others. Smiles, thank you's, kind words and the purchase of my books, easily made me tingle from head to toe. The images of bald little kids riding ever so happily on the shoulders of college heroes triggered my tears each and every time they came by.

Sometimes it takes a really bad situation to see how good people can be. On Saturday afternoon at THON™, a Penn State student came up to me and asked, "Are you doing what I think you're doing?" I just nodded my head up and down and began to cry. She said she noticed I was never sitting, and that I had never left. She also noticed I was alone. (It's interesting because this is also how many of the Four Diamonds families feel at times despite being surrounded by so much love.)

I hadn't announced my 48-hour plan at THON™ because I wasn't seeking accolades. It took a very caring girl who was a moraler responsible for other dancers, to see me and see that I received the love I needed to make it through. From that moment on, word spread of my mission and more and more people came by my table with everything from hugs to cookies to enjoyable and uplifting conversation.

On Sunday morning when I was disoriented and thought I wanted to quit, that moraler simply would not allow it. On Sunday afternoon, when I could not walk without limping on both legs because my feet were swollen and blistered, that moraler helped me to the first aid area. I never would have made it through the 48 hours without her. (This is one of the many examples of unsung heroes at THON™. Exhaustion tends to override memory, leaving people frustrated over desperately wanting to thank someone who helped them, but not knowing their identity.)

THON™ is proof that love can conquer any challenge. I hope you find something to love from this story and deem it worthy of adding to your life, and sharing with another, especially a child. I hope love can warm the hearts of people like the Carrano family who mourn the loss of their lovely little Lauren. I hope love will heal the little boy Darien, who placed a smiley-faced, purple-heart sticker on my heart at THON™. Darien hopes that one day soon, he and all kids will be free from their battles with cancer.

"Hope Surrounds Us" is a new theme for THON™. I know it is true. I also know it is an honor for me to celebrate Penn State students in this book for the love and time they give to keep alive the tradition that *Diamonds Are a Child's Best Friend."* I hope I have helped them to feel proud and inspired.

The following is something I wrote that came to me as I stood in awe in watching what THON™ represents.

The
Honest efforts
Of Penn State students who know
No limits to love…

For the Kids!

I will end this tribute with perhaps the greatest endorsement of THON™, and all that the students do for the Four Diamonds families beyond their extraordinary fundraising efforts. Every year, many of the families return for the event. You'll see those who have been freed of childhood cancer, those who are still dealing with it, and even those who lost a child to cancer.

Len and Judy Hoch, and their three children, Katie, 9, Carley, 5, and Kendall, 3, are just one of the families who never miss THON™. "I know it may sound dumb," admits Judy, "but every year, I'm always looking for Colby, the adorable bald and brown-eyed kid. I always see him in someone's face. Always."

Please visit www.thon.org.

The little Hero's Journey

The sun was beaming with a smile matching mine, early on the pristine fall morning. I was particularly excited about beginning the week as I parked in front of the elementary school where I was doing a five-day author-in-residence program. Like a kid on Christmas morning, I was already anticipating the countless hugs I would enjoy with the children, and all of the loving and inspirational words I would say to them. It was going to be quite a week all right, a week filled with sharing love, laughter, and lessons.

As I opened my car door . . . BAM! My dream week was shattered before it even began. The culprit was a woman. She never touched my car. She never spoke to me. Nonetheless, she crashed into my heart and dented my spirit.

I could hear and feel the woman's wrath as she stormed past me, tongue lashing the 7- or 8-year old boy she was walking to school. The little guy was trailing a few feet behind her. I never did get a good look at his face, but I could see his head was facing straight down. No, it wasn't just his book bag he was carrying, but the heavy load of shattered little feelings.

I stood there stunned as the woman loaded up to deliver one final blow as the boy entered school. "And DON'T wear those pants anymore" she shouted. "What did I tell you about that? They're too short. You look STUPID!"

How could someone be so cruel to a child? I was haunted by thoughts of what an awful start it was to his school day. Would it be any wonder if that boy sought attention, got into trouble, or had trouble learning?

I've often said being sensitive is my greatest gift and my weakest link. Hence, I just couldn't get that scene out of my head. Believing everything happens for a reason, I questioned why I was the sole witness of the pre-school punishment.

Shortly thereafter, hundreds of 2nd, 3rd and 4th graders gathered in the gym for my speech. They heard a much different talk than was planned. I was supposed to explain the weeklong creative writing project they were going to do with me. The theme of their writing was to recognize heroes in their lives. Hopefully, I'd get the students pumped up to give their best effort.

Instead, my talk was more about things like the nasty gash I had on my face from shaving. I realized the cut was a gift and used it as a sign for every boy and girl to see how even a big strong guy like me still gets hurt.

I told the children, *"In one hand we all hold our desire to be seen, heard and appreciated for who we really are. In the other hand, we have our terror of being hurt or rejected. And, take it from me, if you try to throw one of these issues away, it only comes back at you hard and fast, just like a boomerang!"* So, *we spend our entire lives constantly trying to balance these two things.* It clicked. The kids got it, and led me to try something I'd never done before.

I asked for all of the children who could see a hero in the mirror to stand up. To my surprise, probably half of the children did. I think a number of them did so because they thought they were going to be the ones called upon by me.

Instead, I spoke to all of the seated children. I asked, *"Will every one of the children still seated, please raise your hand if you've already had your feelings hurt this morning? Not yesterday or last week, just this morning."* (I was hoping, somehow, the boy I saw before school was one of them). Much to my dismay, a large number of little hands were raised in the air. Sadly, it wasn't even 9:30 A.M., but already many children had fresh wounds.

I asked these children to keep their hands in the air and to go inside themselves for a big decision. I told them, "There is no good or bad here. There is no right or wrong. Nobody has to do anything they don't want to do. I choked up as I told them, *"I want you to know that I'm really sorry you've been hurt. I'm here today and I want to help you. So, if you feel brave in this moment and you think this may be your time to finally see the hero in your mirror, I'd like for you hurting little angels to stand up now with your hands still in the air."*

What probably lasted only a matter of seconds, felt to me like an hour. No one stood. My own fears were triggered as I thought I failed the children and hit a dead end. Then, it happened. A handful of heroes were born.

Their little bodies rose to stand so tall, so proud and yet still, so scared. *"You did it!"* I told them. *"You balanced the struggle I just taught you!"* I then opened my arms as wide as they would stretch and said, *"Okay gang, way to go! All of you come up to the stage here with me!"*

The room was buzzing as they walked to the front. I had the children in the audience sit down, and congratulated them for already being able to see the hero in their mirror. I also thanked them for their heroic deed in leading the way for their fellow students.

Somehow, I couldn't continue without offering one last chance at bravery. I asked, *"Is there anyone left who can't see a hero in the mirror but were too afraid to raise their hand?"* Immediately, another five hands were raised. Again, I opened my arms and said, *"Come on up here with me!"* As you might have guessed, they practically ran to the stage!

Other than me, no one in the gym knew what I was doing. Not the faculty members. Not the children in the audience, and certainly not the group of the more than a dozen new heroes.

I grabbed a little chair and placed it beside me. I then found a volunteer from the fairly even mix of boy and girl heroes, and lifted her so she stood on the chair right next to me. The crowd was giggling at the sight. With my arm around the shoulders of this precious, fragile little angel, I let everyone in on the secret. *"Okay y'all, guess what we going to do now! We are going to help Emily to find the hero in her mirror. I'm now going to call on boys or girls who want to share something they like or admire about Emily."*

Little hands were waving everywhere! *"She's nice." "She's a good friend." "She shares." "She helps me."* It didn't matter that the comments were basically the same for all of the new little heroes. What matters is children learned how to give and receive, in a rare public showing of unconditional love and support. What matters is these little heroes tapped into the courage and balance we all need to fulfill our hopes and dreams. What matters is they truly believed these compliments, lighting up the room with the big smiles on their little faces! Before lifting each new hero off the chair, I asked him or her to repeat the great qualities others saw in them. Amazingly, they all could, easily.

Later, I even stood a teacher on the same little chair and he soaked up praise from the kids like he was "Sponge Bob Square Pants." (See Nickelodeon if you don't get the reference!). I then created more of a ruckus by giving a homework assignment to all the teachers. We had to take five minutes of my Hero Writing workshop with each class for students to share why they felt their teacher was a hero. There were a number of crying teachers that week. I even got a step stool for "placing people on a pedestal." I now carry it with me to every school I visit.

I celebrate that first brave little hero for his journey into school on that pristine fall morning. I write this story as a way to thank him for being a divine instrument in my life. He guided me and inspired me to create a more powerful week with the children than I ever dreamed. Heroes are everywhere and so are life's lessons. Remember this always as you go through life on your own unique Hero's or Heroine's Journey.

The "I's" Have It

Say *I Love You* and mean it every chance you get.

Savor every time a child says, *"I Love You."*

Remember what is really important really is.

Remember what isn't really important really isn't.

Include a child in decisions that involve them.

Teach a child there is no "I" in team.

Train a child to listen to their intuition and inner voice.

Encourage a child to be independent.

Encourage a child's imagination.

Encourage a child's individuality.

Insist on proper manners.

Protect the innocence of a child.

Don't ignore issues and problems hoping they'll disappear.

Have a child scratch an itch for you.

Give love when you scratch an itch for a child.

Keep updated forms of personal identification for a child.

Have a life insurance policy.

Get the best health insurance you can.

Acknowledge and encourage a child's good ideas.

Support a child's healthy interests.

Teach a child there is always time and room for improvement.

Make an impact with a child despite never being able to measure it.

Going To Bat For Rebecca

Rebecca is my gorgeous little friend on the front cover. "My favorite all-time Rebecca story," says her dad Mike, "is when my wife Libby, and our dear friend M.C. Antil were with her at a restaurant having dinner. Rebecca asked to be excused. I said 'yes' and the three of us continued talking. I couldn't see what she was doing but M.C. could. His eyes began to well up. I turned around to see Rebecca had walked over to a man having dinner by himself. He was crying, too. She sat with him for twenty minutes. When she returned to our table, the man's cheeks were wet! I asked her what she did. She said, 'I could tell the man was lonely, so I thought he might enjoy some company.' Mike says, "And I guarantee you, she never told that man she couldn't see very well. She was much too concerned about him."

Rebecca's parents see her as "an old soul." "She is very sensitive," says her mom Libby. "Some of the stuff she does and says, I just don't know where it comes from." Dad agrees. "Early on in her, there emerged this spirit, this special way with people. There is something inside of her I don't understand, but I do see it," Mike says.

Rebecca is now 11. She is a girl with great vision *for* life, but far from great eyesight *in* life. "I was in first grade when I took a vision test," she recalls more than four years later. "The chart was across the room and when I got to the middle, I couldn't read it. My mom told me to stop kidding around, and I said, 'I'm not. I can't.'"

Rebecca was immediately diagnosed with retinitis pigmentosa, a disease that causes the cells in the retina to degenerate and die. RP begins with decreased night vision. It then takes away peripheral vision. The rate of decline and the degree of it varies in individuals due to genetic makeup. Many retain a small degree of central vision. "It was just flat out shock," says Rebecca's mother Libby. "Depression. There's no way to describe the horror of it."

Rebecca went through hours of tests that day. Libby says draw-ing blood made Rebecca "insane," and that her daughter was still crying when they left the hospital near their home in South Car-olina. "When we walked outside, talking about her Band-Aid, we saw a little girl with her father. She was sitting in a wagon. I no-ticed the girl had a pump in her hand. Her father told us she was eight-years old and just had her third open heart surgery. I believe God sticks in front of you what you need to see. What Rebecca has is not life threatening, but it sure is life altering."

Libby was so upset that it took two broken crowns for her to notice how much she was grinding her teeth. "I couldn't talk in front of Rebecca, and Mike was already in a negative situation with his job, so I couldn't unload much on him. I would cry every time I'd be driving alone."

Libby added, "Shortly after she was first diagnosed, I walked outside to watch the sunset. When the sun sets in the marsh where we are, you can't see the water, but there are these really intense colors that are just so amazing and beautiful. I stood there crying and said to myself, 'Rebecca is not going to see this.'"

For a while, going to sleep was scary for Rebecca. "I was afraid I would wake up blind," she said. Her father, who usually reacts with humor, had only disbelief. "It's surreal. It's so horrible," he says.

Rebecca has a brother "Night Train," who is 16. He is Mike's son from a previous marriage. She spells their last name "V as in Vic-tor, double E, C, K." Their famous grandfather used to explain it quite differently. He joked, "It's Veeck, as in wreck!" To even a non-baseball fan, the Veeck name might sound familiar. Two of the most creative and controversial promoters in the history of professional sports are Rebecca's grandfather, Bill, and her father, Mike.

Bill Veeck, Jr. was a rebel owner who lived by his saying, "Tra-dition is the albatross around the neck of progress." In 1951, he introduced a midget into the major leagues as a pinch hitter. 3'7" Eddie Gaedel who wore number 1/8 on his St. Louis Browns jer-sey, walked on four pitches and then promptly walked out of base-ball as a celebrity and its only little person player. Bill Veeck's other attendance-generating ideas included fireworks, names on the back of uniforms, putting ivy on the walls of Wrigley Field, Bat

Day, and You Be The Manager Night. He also signed Larry Doby, the American League's first black player, and baseball's oldest rookie, 43-year old Satchel Paige, the Negro League legend.

Bill lost his right leg as a marine in the South Pacific during World War II. He underwent 37 operations as a result of complications. He had emphysema and lung cancer, too. Five years after his death, Bill Veeck, Jr. was elected into the Baseball Hall of Fame in 1991. It was also the year Rebecca was born. "If you take my hand and hold it across the bridge of her nose, you will see my father," claims Mike. "He had blonde hair, blue eyes, and that same strength and determination. I have never heard either of them say, 'I hurt. I'm having a bad day.'"

In comparing Mike Veeck to his father, baseball people know "The apple didn't fall from the tree." Most also believe the apple must have landed on Mike's head, too. When other teams were doing Wedding Night stunts, he did Divorce Night. He signed Ila Borders, the first woman to play professional baseball with men. Mike's 1979 Disco Demolition Night promotion with the Chicago White Sox is legendary. The event drew a huge turnout and made headlines all right. Literally thousands stormed the field at Comiskey Park for the blowing up of disco records. The ensuing riot caused the fourth forfeit in major league history, and caused Mike to get fired by his dad.

In 1990, the year before Rebecca was born, Mike hired Don Wardlow as radio announcer for the Miami Miracle minor league team. What was unusual about that? Don Wardlow was born without eyes. For most of the time since then, Mike Veeck has employed him as an announcer for minor league teams he runs. "I hired the first blind announcer," he says. "How ironic is that?"

It wasn't long after Rebecca was diagnosed with retinitis pigmentosa, that Mike's vision didn't involve working for the Tampa Bay Devil Rays. His idea was to travel. "It came from something my mom told me because we have very few surviving photos of all of us together. (Mike was one of six kids.) "My mom said we were too busy living in the moment to take photos. She said we keep postcards in our heads of all our wonderful experiences. Since travel is the hobby that has given me the most joy, I wanted to pass that wanderlust and those kinds of postcards on to Rebecca."

Further inspiration for getting the family show on the road goes to Libby. Mike says, "She told me our lives were going to change, and if I wanted to continue to be a man driven by my career, I could. However, I was going to miss something. I was often an absent father with Night Train, so I didn't want it to happen again." "We took a year and were constantly traveling, trying to show her everything," adds Libby.

Rebecca's parents took her on a year-long tour. They went to U.S. National Parks. They did things like visit a pistachio tree farm, and stop in the middle of magnificent rose gardens so Rebecca could not only see the beauty of them, but could also appreciate the intense smell. The journey was a loving race against time, led by parents who wanted their daughter to see as many things as possible, and to have as wide a frame of reference as possible before she lost her eyesight.

Libby recalls a powerful moment for Rebecca came in California when they stumbled upon a former camp for Japanese prisoners that Mike recognized from years ago. "It looks like a trailer park but has markers for people, a monument, and children's graves. She was very intrigued."

"We started in the summer after second grade," says Rebecca. "I have been to 32 states. South Carolina is one of my favorite states. So are California, New York, Maryland, and Florida. Bermuda is breathtakingly beautiful. I loved Guadalajara in Mexico, and horseback riding in Death Valley was fun, too."

Mike admits, "We put the top down on the car, and I let Rebecca sit on my lap and drive down the Pacific Coast Highway. We jumped a fence and picked almonds. We picked cotton. We have things like rocks, and a piece of bark from a giant sequoia. We brought all these things home and put them into an overflowing memory box for Rebecca. It is a constant source of joy and fun." Rebecca says, "My memory box is my most important possession."

"I didn't care if Rebecca missed 150 days of school," Mike says, "but it was great how the long journey stopped." Libby saw the situation clearly. "We realized she is just a little girl who wants to be with her classmates, too. She needs that socialization and support we can't provide. All the travel was pushing her too much so we slowed it down."

Mike, Rebecca, and Libby Veeck in Mexico.

Rebecca agrees. "It was really cool, but sometimes you want to stay home. It's really nice because I get to be with my friends and just enjoy every minute of my breathing moments. I think we should take the moment as we live it. Don't try to ask what you're going to be doing in the future."

Rebecca's views of the future and present are different from her parents. "My vision has been stable," she claims. "My peripheral is great around the middle. I can see the baseball fields and the scoreboards a bit, too. My own definition is, I can see everything but little print in books. That can be really despairing, triple despairing."

Rebecca's mother sees it this way. "It's tough," admits Libby. "We think she has blind spots in her central vision, and she may be working with one little corner of her peripheral. Overall, she maneuvers around the house very well, but sometimes she bumps into things or us. If I send her to go look for something in her room, sometimes she'll be fifteen or twenty minutes. Then, I'll go up and find it right away. What she lacks in some areas, she makes up for in others. That child certainly has no lack of hearing. You can whisper and she'll bust you!"

Mike says, "The problem is we self-diagnose all the time. Rebecca tells us there are just gray spots, but I have nothing to compare it to, though she is asking for help much more in the last six months. Sometimes now, she'll reach for my cheek before kissing me in the morning as she leaves for school."

These differing family views of Rebecca's vision are cause for celebration. They are based on listening and respect, not a lack of communication! "We don't really talk about it," says Rebecca, "because I prefer it that way. My parents help me so much by not pushing me into talking about it. If they want to talk about my eyes, they always ask permission, and I think that's very important. Sometimes, they think they're not good parents, but I know I'm lucky to have them. My dad lets me help at the ballpark and is teaching me how to run the team, even if there is a child labor law. My mom teaches me how to sew and cook. They teach me wise little ways and give me advice. They're just really good friends."

"We are kind of a goofy family," laughs Libby. "We're certainly not very *Cleaver-esque* at all. There is the adult-child thing, but there's definitely much more of a buddy system around here."

Mike says, "I never lose sight of the fact that no matter how mom or dad feels, Rebecca is the one who has this affliction. No matter how tough it gets, it is paramount to keep that in the forefront of my thinking or it would dishonor the respect and admiration I have for her and had for my father. She deals with difficulty so well, just like my father. I thought I was going to teach her. Instead, I hold her hand and hope it rubs off."

Regardless of whose view of Rebecca's vision is most accurate, the family agrees that nothing stops this child from living, dreaming, and celebrating fully. Rebecca loves magic and mermaids and wants to write books about them. She loves writing so much that she has kept a journal since she was six.

On Mondays and Saturdays, she has piano lessons. After four months, Rebecca's teacher says she is her shining star. On Wednesdays, she rides horses. "I'm a good rider," boasts Rebecca. "I've done walk, trot, and canter around the ring. The next step after getting my gallop good is to jump!" "I can't even go there and watch," says her mother.

Rebecca collects American Girl dolls, and wants to get back into karate or dance. "I've done ballet and want to do tap. I know the Fox Trot, the Cha Cha, the Charleston, the Shag, and the Waltz," she says. "Yeah, I sure have done a lot, but there is just so much to do and you never know what's going to happen in life so you get it all in as soon as you can."

School is now tougher on Rebecca than in the past. For middle school, she is being driven to become completely independent using Braille and an abacus. "Learning Braille is like a second language, but really it's like my fourth. I speak French, some Spanish, Japanese, and Latin, too." Rebecca notes she can do just about anything on Braille since she started learning it in first grade. She also points out that her classmates are the greatest. Her father is filled with joy watching the special bond of Libby reading to Rebecca for one hour every night.

Rebecca plans to attend college. She dreams of acting on Broadway or in movies. She dreams of living on a ranch with a beautiful, well-built barn for ten horses, even though she will only have five. She also plans to be right at home like her father and grandfather by owning minor league baseball teams. "The person who creates the atmosphere is the one who makes it fun. It's all about the fans. Always."

Mike Veeck now enjoys his own dream job as an executive marketing genius for the Detroit Tigers. Despite the heartache of thinking it was his last shot at the major leagues, he twice turned down positions with the team since their family was staying in South Carolina and he would not be away from Libby and Rebecca.

Dave Dombrowski, the Tigers' President and CEO, would simply not allow strike three. When he so compassionately offered to structure the deal anyway necessary, it changed Mike's life. "I never knew that was possible. I finally made a selfless decision and thought about giving to Rebecca and Libby first. Suddenly, when I tried the best a person can, to do the right thing, the reward was so much bigger than all those years when I was selfish, and scratching and clawing."

As for their view of the future, Libby and Mike are in somewhat of a balancing act. On one hand, they're hoping to hold off the inevitable. On the other, they are eager and optimistic for the future to arrive. "I do believe with every bone in my body that there will be a cure," Mike says. An optimistic Rebecca adds, "The doctor says I might have Stargardt (Macular Dystrophy), which is a slower process than RP. They say it's probably five years out before they have a cure for both diseases. But if I go blind, I go blind. Who cares? It's just there, and it's all I can expect. It's not the end of the world. Other people have worse stuff than I do."

At the end of this book, I share why it is so special for me to celebrate Rebecca on the book's cover. This girl who loves Greek Mythology is a little Goddess to me. She and her parents never sound like "Veeck as in victim." They are "Veeck as in valiant." For these reasons and more, it is an honor to celebrate them. "One thing you hear often in our house is, 'We have much to be thankful for,'" says Mike. If they could, Libby and Mike Veeck would give their eyes to Rebecca. Since they can't, they always find ways make her see how much they like, love, respect, and celebrate her.

Perhaps this story will move you to take a look into the Foundation Fighting Blindness www.blindness.org. When a cure for her condition comes one day soon, we will celebrate "Veeck as in victory." Oh, what a promotion Mike will create then! Until that time, there is plenty of room on the team for anyone and everyone interested in *going to bat for Rebecca.*

Going to bat for Rebecca on the beach in Bermuda.

This Land Is Your Land

Celebrate a child by celebrating the gift of freedom he or she enjoys. Celebrate a child by providing them with experiences to taste all that America has to offer.

Mike Veeck has! Rebecca's dad has been to all fifty states. Mine eyes have seen the glory of 48 of them as only the beauty and wonders of Montana and Alaska have eluded me to this point. I can't wait to complete my American crusade and feel like I'm saving two of the greatest states for last!

America is such an amazingly diverse country, it saddens me that so many citizens take it for granted. I wonder, "How can you *not* want to see this great land of ours?" How can you not share this patriotic spirit with a child? This land really is your land.

I firmly believe one of the best ways to appreciate America is to leave it. If being in a foreign land doesn't help you to see how good we have it, then it's entirely possible you may never get it. I like very much to see the world, but I love returning home to the United States of America.

Remember, "Stand beside her and guide her" begins with you. If you do want to help yourself and a child to love more about America, you may be helped by checking out a couple of fun and cool books authored by some of my All-American friends:

MY AMERICA: *What My Country Means to Me, by 150 Americans from All Walks of Life* by Hugh Downs

1001 Ways to Celebrate America by Antoinette Kuritz and Greg Godek.

This Land Is Your Land

Vote! You'll be teaching a child about patriotism and our precious rights.

Take a child into the voting booth with you.

Encourage mock political elections at schools.

Vote for political candidates who truly support children's causes.

Teach a child to believe in "The American Dream."

Live with good ol' American pride.

Teach a child respect for the flag.

Share American history with a child.

Teach a child respect for our armed forces.

Teach a child respect for police officers.

Teach a child respect for firefighters.

Teach a child respect for emergency medical personnel.

Remember the "memorial" part on Memorial Day.

Teach a child respect for the freedom of speech of others.

Visit the Tomb of the Unknown Soldier.

Take a child on a tour of The White House.

Take a child to the Smithsonian Institute.

Take child to see the Lincoln Memorial.

Take a child on a tour of your state capitol.

Teach a child the words to our National Anthem.

Keep a child away from dangerous fireworks.

Read Dr. Martin Luther King's "I Have a Dream" speech to a child.

Celebrate a child by experiencing some of my personal favorite U.S. (unbelievable sites):

Bask in the bloom of the azaleas during spring in Augusta, Georgia.

Walk through downtown in the "Windy City" of Chicago.

Race to Churchill Downs in Louisville for the running of The Kentucky Derby.

Gawk at the Grand Canyon.

Color yourself lucky seeing the breathtaking rainbows over Hilo, Hawaii.

Get turned on by the lights of Las Vegas at night.

Look for the moose still on the loose in Maine.

Make your way down 17-mile drive in the Monterey Peninsula.

Know there is nothing in the world like New York City.

Fixate on Niagara Falls.

Pack your belongings for a trip on the Pacific Coast Highway.

Soothe your soul in the gorgeous red rock region of Sedona, Arizona.

Catch the Cathedral of St. John the Divine in Manhattan.

Invite yourselves to Independence Mall in Philadelphia.

Revel in the Rocky Mountains.

Get to Graceland and Beal Street in Memphis.

Hang out at Baltimore's Inner Harbor.

Stare at the Statue of Liberty.

Go anywhere down south to enjoy good ol' "Southern Hospitality."

Hang out anywhere in the Heartland of America.

The Kids' New Battle Of Gettysburg

Okay, maybe I'm a bit slow when it comes to grasping certain concepts. One example is, for the life of me, I just can't understand the tragic moment in U.S. history we call "The Civil War. How the word "civil" can be used with the word "war" is beyond me. I don't see anything civil about people killing each other in cold blood.

Therefore, seven score (140 years) after President Abraham Lincoln delivered his infamous Gettysburg Address; it gives me great pride to take you back to historic Gettysburg, to a battlefield where victory was achieved *with* love. There were no deaths, no wounded, and no missing. In fact, the only confirmed casualty was a stolen cell phone. (More on that later.)

"The Kids' New Battle of Gettysburg" was fought on the grounds of the James Gettys Elementary School. It is located just a few miles from the famous battlefield and the home of President Dwight D. Eisenhower. Both "Honest Abe" and "Ike" would have liked the story of the children's mission I'm going to share with you, and they would have been damn proud of the fine young Americans involved.

This mission was called, *"Children Loving Children: Making Dreams Come True."* The real battle here was . . . there was no real battle plan for helping children. More importantly, there was no money either.

Nonetheless, leading the charge was a trio of third-grade girls, Alison Stoner, 9, Signe Carlson, 9, and Felicia Orendorff, 8. The war in Afghanistan was upsetting them. They were concerned for the safety of Afghan children. The first shot fired was when Allie said, "We've got to do something."

While tossing around a red ball on the school playground, the girls came up with some interesting ideas. They originally thought of asking for enough money to get a Barbie doll to send to Afghanistan.

Thomas with Alison Stoner, Felicia Orendorff, and Signe Carlson at the official start of the battle.

Members of "Team Jessica" posing behind her at the battle's end.
Photo by Mark Garvin.

Having no guarantee it would work, the idea never made it out of the box. Allie also wanted to feed the Afghan children. She said, "I heard the kids over there have to eat bats and bugs and stuff. I don't think that's right." Once the cafeteria workers told the girls the school doesn't waste food, this idea was taken off the menu, too.

The girls enlisted the help of their teacher, Marsha Boehner, a loving woman with more than 20 years of experience in the class-room. This is a teacher who encourages students daily with com-ments such as "Think BIG! Don't think little." Naturally, Boehner supported the girls, but says she told them, "You need a plan." Boehner said, "9-11 affected the children very much, but these are kind, warm souls anyway. They held a class meeting and voted on a list of ideas. It evolved into helping a child here in America who didn't attend our school."

When the School Principal Ted Gilbert, a very nurturing man himself, learned of the third grade class project, he suggested they contact me to help with fundraising. I met Ted a few months ear-lier while signing books at Penn State's THON event. He showed his teacher a copy of my first book, *KIDS RULE! The Hopes and Dreams of 21st Century Children*. Ms. Boehner then shared the book with her class. Allie claims they said, "Why don't we contact this dude? So, we did."

I received an e-mail from the girls. It was such a pleasant sur-prise; I immediately replied that I would help. After a few more e-mails were exchanged, I learned that not only was their teacher involved, but also the project had grown school-wide (kinder-garten through third-grade).

First, I set out to find the perfect child in need. I wanted to pro-tect the Gettysburg children and guarantee the outcome. It felt im-portant to me that their first major experience in giving be positive. If so, the children might continue to be givers and could hopefully inspire others to do the same. Also, I couldn't bear for their hard-earned money to go to a parent who would misuse it on alcohol, drugs, or something else that would break their little hearts if word ever reached them.

I enlisted the help of Dave Willauer, Principal at the Royersford Elementary School, more than 100 miles east of Gettysburg in the suburbs of Philadelphia. "King David" as I call him, happens to be a minister and a hero of mine. He later said, "As the administrator of the school, my first instinct was protecting the privacy and dignity of the needy child. Yet, I knew I had to make this thing happen. The chain of the events the children had started was already at work. I believe God gave me a role to play. Was I going to stand in the way or be a part of the process? I just had to keep it going."

The king consulted with guidance counselor, Ginny Prevost. Quickly, they found our queen. Her name was Jessica, a ten-year old fourth-grader from a family of nine, who lived in an apartment near the school. "Unfortunately, we have plenty of needy kids at our school," said Willauer. "We selected Jessica because of the past level of appreciation she showed for people reaching out to her. It never mattered what it was, when you gave something to Jessica, it was always just so appreciated."

When I went to ask permission for Jessica to be the recipient, her parents agreed, but were totally speechless. They were simply amazed it was a group of third-graders I was representing in such a random act of kindness. I gave a written homework assignment to Jessica. I asked her to tell the little Gettysburgers something about herself. Here is what she wrote:

> Hi! My name is Jessica G. and I got the chance for Mr. Baldrick to talk with me about you students. I am ten years old in the fourth grade. I really <u>Love</u> to read and play soccer. I have 9 people in my family. What I would really want to have are those sneakers that turn into roller skates. If you get them, I am a size $5\frac{1}{2}$. My family could use a computer.
>
> I thank you so much for doing this for me. It is so nice of you. But I think you are doing the right thing. I never thought I would be the one picked for something like this. My family could also use a couple of boxes of Band-Aids. Once again, I thank you for your kindness to me.
>
> From, Jessica G.

The third-graders were touched. Felicia Orendorff said, "The letter was very convincing. It made Allie cry. It made me feel good that we were helping her." Signe Carlson added, "It made me feel nice because I'm not always a good friend, but we were being a good friend to Jessica."

The little troops were nervous but inspired. All they had to do was raise the money. A goal of $1,100 was established. I told the girls it would be easier to get people to give money, if they gave them something in return. Therefore, I offered them 100 copies of my first book, *KIDS RULE! The Hopes and Dreams of 21st Century Children.*

I joined the girls to launch the two-week book drive. The local daily newspaper, *The Gettysburg Times* even covered the event. In a classy and caring gesture, reporter Kami Masemer and photographer Darryl Wheeler promised to run the story the next day saying, "We want to do everything we can to help the children succeed. Maybe our story can drum up a little business for them."

Kids ate lunch at a table in the school lobby. Some even stood near the road in front of the school holding up copies of the book to passing traffic. Business was so brisk that the drive came to an early halt. In only one week, the children raised $1,664. "It was wonderful," said Ms. Boehner. "It was like I had these little caterpillars before, and now I have these beautiful little butterflies flying around. The children really came out during this project and became these self-assured, determined, loving little business people."

The mission for Jessica quickly grew into a movement. A local family donated a computer. Wal*Mart kindly matched our efforts with a $1,000 pledge. Johnson & Johnson offered a gift package with Band-Aids and other products. The Trappe Book Center gave us a huge discount so we took Jessica on a book-buying spree. It was a total team effort.

One mother was moved and surprised by her son, Matthew's willingness to help. For the first time, the little boy took money from his piggy bank. He gave it to The Jessica Fund, and she claimed he's never done anything like that before.

Ms. Boehner and I did our shopping for Jessica at Wal*Mart, in appreciation of their support. We were able to buy her the things she wanted...and more. We got her a desk, chair, a variety of computer games and accessories, and a $250 gift certificate. *(Author's note: I hope the person who stole my cell phone during this goodwill shopping mission knows it troubled me deeply.)*

After being on both ends of the cash register, the only thing left to do was share the joy with Jessica. For a few reasons, the plan was for me to handle the presentation. All parties involved wanted to honor the privacy of Jessica's family. We also wanted to teach the children that in a true act of giving, it is done without attachment to the outcome. However, in our hearts, and in the back of our minds, we all hoped Jessica would want to meet her donors. What a gift it was in return that she did!

King David arranged for a Saturday afternoon pizza and gift-giving party for Jessica at Royersford Elementary. (His heir to the throne, son Matt, kindly assembled the computer desk.) Ted Gilbert, Marsha Boehner, Alison Stoner, Ashley Harpster, Felicia Orendorff and Felicia's mom, made the three-hour drive. Jessica's mom was on hand, too.

Somehow, the children created the spirit of Christmas in June. They bonded and giggled as little girls do, while the grownups in attendance were moved to tears. Ms. Boehner said, "It was so fun to watch the children. They were so tender and charming together." Ted Gilbert was equally proud saying, "This reminds me of a TV show called 'Queen for a Day' that I used to watch as a kid. This was a truly special moment." The host Principal said he stood in awe, enjoying his role as a spectator.

Dave Willauer said, "The thing that impressed me was the connection that took place, and it was a connection on a whole lot of levels. The girls actually saw someone else in need that they were helping. They knew Jessica's life went on before they met, and they knew it would go on after they had gone. But they also knew they had an opportunity to change it. That is a lesson they will take with them forever."

After the party, I drove Jessica home. Believe me, she was not simply appreciative. This day, she was one completely overwhelmed little girl. Jessica just kept saying, "Thank you. Thank you. Thank you. I am so happy and feel so very, very special."

(Author's note: Not only were many hearts warmed by this project, but the leftover funds were used to buy coats to warm needy children during the cold winters in Gettysburg, PA.)

Nine for Nine

Most of the civilized world has heard about the QueCreek Nine. They were the trapped coal miners in Somerset, PA during the summer of 2002. Newscasts near and far kept the world on edge as a rescue team of 200 worked around the clock for more than three days in the hopes of saving nine lives.

An accidental unleashing of millions of gallons of water from the nearby Saxman Mine turned the coal-filled workspace known as the QueCreek Mine, into a flooded and terrifying underground hell. The dangerous and tedious rescue mission was like fighting blindfolded through 240 feet of rock to extract nine people from the bottom of a pool. Oh yeah, for a number of reasons it was also a daring race against the clock.

I know some people think the QueCreek Nine have cashed in by selling their stories. Their book and TV movie were released within four months. But, I too have a tale to tell about the Que-Creek Mine Rescue that is uniquely mine. It is based on my own observations as a TV journalist on the scene, as well as lessons I learned that week on leadership and teaching by example. I hope you find this story offers a host of ways to teach a child and help them to celebrate this wonderful thing we call "life."

The media mob, of which I was a member, was set up at a shopping plaza a few miles from the mine. Only a small, rotating pool of journalists, print, radio, and one TV camera person were bused in every few hours to get coverage of the rescue from a safe distance up the hill. Upon the journalists' return to the media area, any new pictures, sound, and quotes had to be shared. No live coverage was permitted.

When it was discovered that all nine miners were alive, David LaTorre, (Press Secretary for Pennsylvania Governor Mark Schweiker) and other officials (even the families) agreed America *needed* to see the end of the rescue, live on TV. Working for ABC News, I was then selected by my peers from all TV networks to establish and oversee the live coverage. We had less than one hour to be ready for the world to watch. It was a once-in-a-lifetime thrill that came with an over-whelming sense of pressure and responsibility.

I was the only TV reporter live on the scene when the nine miners were miraculously rescued. The experience was an honor, and a gift, I shall never forget. It is really hard to explain the impact of being right there, when nine men whom many presumed dead, were brought out alive, healthy, thirsty for beer, and hungry for donuts or any other food they could get their filthy hands on.

You can tell any child I earned that privilege by showing respect, thinking creatively, and being fair as well as professional. In covering the story, I took a pro-active approach in convincing the network TV outlets on site that we could all do a better job if we worked together. This was due to the uniqueness of the situation and limited access we faced. Often, I represented the TV media in dealings with government and law enforcement officials in charge of the scene. I was also quite vocal in establishing a TV code of ethics, so we could agree to what we would do, and more impor-tantly, what we wouldn't do in covering the story.

I learned some valuable life lessons from covering the miracle rescue, and now share them whenever I give speeches. Audience responses have been so positive that people have suggested I write about the lessons. I agreed to do so for this book, especially since the messages can be taught to inspire children that attitude can tri-umph over adversity.

HOPE. Many think of denial as a negative term, but denial can be a powerful tool in protecting us from pain until we are ready to deal with it. Sometimes, we are so afraid of even admitting denial, that we completely hide behind this intangible thing we call hope. Other times, hope is partnered with the power of faith. However it was used, hope was all we had during the painstakingly long 77-hours the miners were trapped.

When Bob Long, an engineering technician, came up with the life-saving idea of pumping warm air down to the miners, an educated guess had to be made as to where exactly they might be trapped. Even though he used thousands of dollars worth of GPS equipment to make his decision, no one knew the perfect guess for placement of the air had been made. All we had was hope.

When the huge drill bit broke trying to break through the earth, it was a crushing blow to foreman, John Hamilton, and his crew. Replacement parts had to be located, then rushed in from West Virginia. During the nearly half-day wait for the drilling to resume, the rescue workers, friends, family, and the rest of us watching, felt helpless, but definitely not hopeless.

For most of the 77-hours they were trapped, the nine miners were in the dark about being rescued. Though they used their battery-operated lights sparingly, none of them had to look very hard to see fear on the other eight faces. Each man prepared to die. They even considered picking the way they'd prefer to perish. Drowning and suffocating were their most likely choices. The miners wrote farewell notes and hung them in an airtight white bucket so they would be easily found. They did this to let go of their loved ones. But never did the nine let go of hope.

We always have hope. No matter how difficult it seems or how tough it actually gets, miracles do happen every single day. We see it. We know it. And so, we must believe. We must always have hope. Children who see hope in grownups, children who are taught hope, will always have it themselves when they need it most.

TEAMWORK/HARD WORK. The rescue operation was a winning show of teamwork, despite the fact that so many factions were involved. The fellow miners of the QueCreek Nine led the way in an undying display of dedication and determination. There were also mining experts from the industry, from the U.S. Department of Labor, and from the Pennsylvania Department of Environmental Protection. Pennsylvania Governor Mark Schweiker's staff was actively involved, as was the Pennsylvania State Police. Even the U.S. Navy played a key role in the efforts.

This was one difficult situation in which to be upbeat. Yet, seemingly, everyone was. At the time, the United States was grasping for more than a positive attitude from a united group of rescue workers. A positive outcome was a must! If you recall, the Que-Creek mining accident took place only ten months after 9-11, and it was only ten miles from where Flight 93 crashed in Shanksville, PA. Raising nine miners in body bags would have been devastating to our nation.

Every person who was at the fantastic finale was exhausted, physically, mentally and emotionally. Only you never would have known it. Smiles, hugs, high five's, and tears of joy were everywhere I looked. If you caught any of my live interviews with rescue officials Joe Sbaffoni, David Hess, Dave Lauriski or Governor Schweiker, their comments on the effort proved convincingly that the taste of success is never sweeter than when teamwork is involved. Having others with whom to share the experience is far more gratifying than any individual achievement.

Working as a team offers the best chance for the best result because you have more great minds, more hands on deck, and more emotional support than when going it alone. Checking one's ego at the door and working in tandem means everyone receives credit for a job well done. The whole is only as great as the sum of its parts.

Regardless of the outcome, teamwork was never an issue in the rescue of the miners. Neither was hard work. 240-feet of rock hard earth surrendered before any of the miners or their rescuers did.

LEADERSHIP. Though dealing with a flooded coal mine wasn't in his job description, Pennsylvania Governor Mark Schweiker was a leader in the rescue efforts. It didn't matter he knew as little about mining as I did. He knew about patience and integrity. He knew to listen to the experts. He knew honesty as he handled talking with the media and the families. He valued miners over money. Like a good leader, he did what could be done in an underground rescue that was uphill every step of the way.

Mark Schweiker had been like any other Lieutenant Governor in any other state. He was quietly serving in the elected office for nearly seven years while the decorated war hero, Tom Ridge, was the popular two-time Governor. In October 2001, when President Bush called upon Ridge to assume the newly appointed position as Director of Homeland Security, Mark Schweiker suddenly had to take a big step up, and he had some pretty big shoes to fill.

Even before he officially became the 44th man to be handed the keys to the Keystone State, Schweiker announced he would not run for a second term as Governor, voting instead to spend more time with his wife, Katherine, and their three children, Brett, Eric, and Kara. (That alone is reason enough to celebrate him in this book.)

The new Governor was to simply stay the course. The biggest pothole on his 15-month road to retirement from public office was expected to be the collapse of the poorly managed Philadelphia school system. But it only took a little while for Governor Schweiker to leave a legacy, and it didn't come by rescuing big city schools on shaky ground. It came through the rescue of nine miners trapped deep *underground* in the sleepy little town of Somerset.

The first time I met Mark Schweiker, I literally bumped into him in Somerset. We were both thanking volunteers from the Salvation Army for their great job in support of the rescue team and the working media. He was an unassuming guy wearing a pair of blue jeans and a denim shirt. I liked him from that first brief encounter, and my respect for him has only grown as I've spent time with him.

As Governor, he earned the title of "The Honorable Mark Schweiker." He could have easily made a brief public appearance in Somerset to show concern for the cause. He then could have offered support, and told his staff to keep him informed before returning to the State Capitol in Harrisburg.

Doing what was needed, Mark Schweiker acted more like Pennsylvania's father than its governor. He never left Somerset until it was over (and believe me, if the miners did not come out alive, the governor might have wished there was 240-feet of rock between him and the countless critics there would have been drilling away at his handling of the situation).

Never during the process did I see Mark Schweiker fail to protect the families of the miners and the rescue workers. He treated them by the Golden Rule, as he would have liked to be treated if it was his loved one trapped in the mine.

The Governor wore the same jeans for four straight days. He also placed a revolving door on his private hotel room so many of the rescue workers could shower, sleep, or just chill out in the air conditioning. He tried to update the families every hour, even during the most gut-wrenching times. He made sure they got any information before the media did.

On the night the miners were saved, Mark Schweiker told me privately he had scheduled plans to celebrate his children that night. He had gotten tickets to take them to a rock concert. *"The Who* is my favorite band and I wanted my kids to see them. I was really looking forward to sharing that part of me with them," he said. He told me he apologized to his kids for not being able to go to the show, and that he also asked them to pay close attention to the events in Somerset so they could learn about the greatest example of teamwork he had ever seen.

Every team needs leaders. Every child does, too. Leaders need character, and character is like saving for retirement. The only way you'll have enough when you need it is if you constantly build it along the way.

COURAGE. Between the miners and their rescuers were a rock and a hard place 240 feet thick. Thank goodness there was as much courage in Somerset as there was coal. The trapped miners used it to get to a safe place, and to wait for a rescue they didn't know would happen or be able to reach them in time. The families used courage to count on a miracle, and to survive the ordeal of waiting, wondering, and worrying. The rescue workers used courage to make critical decisions and to overcome the fear of making critical mistakes. There was no book available on Amazon.com titled, "The Flooded Coalmine Rescue Handbook." I checked.

The QueCreek rescue effort was groundbreaking in more ways than one. The officials needed tremendous courage in knowing nine men were looking to them for life, and many more would be looking to pin the blame on them for failure, in ways even faster and more furious than the water that rushed in on the miners.

Yes indeed, there is a thin line between bravery and cowardice. We all have the ability for both inside us. The difference between the two is courage. Courage doesn't mean you don't have fear. Courage means you feel your fear, and choose to continue on your mission in spite of it.

Dealing with fear isn't easy. Although, the more you do deal with your fear, the easier the process can become for you. I say this despite having learned the issue is one of those vicious circles in life, like needing experience to get a good job, and needing a job to get good experience. Simply put, you need courage to deal with your fear.

Here's the way I see the situation. The words "facing your fear" even sound scary. So, maybe it isn't the best term to use. It implies that whatever you're afraid of is right in your face. Many times this is the case, and I don't know about you, but I can't think of too many people I know who can see the world clearly with something right in their face.

I have learned to look at fear differently, and you can, too. I used to be the type who could manufacture rejection so well internally, that there was really no need for me to get rejected by someone else. For example, I could firmly convince myself that an attractive woman would reject me. Therefore, it was silly for me to even consider asking her out for a date. I thought. "Why bother? Why subject myself to unnecessary humiliation?"

One experience at a time, I have improved my ability to choose the freedom of courage over the confinement of fear. I have used courage to look into the mirror to accept both my faults and my finer points. I've assumed ownership of my childhood hurts, and my ability to stop re-creating them. I've walked right through rejection, while at other times gotten back up after I allowed it to knock me down. More than ever, I live by my motto, *"Swing hard in case you hit it!"*

Courage is what enabled me to risk falling flat on my face in front of my peers and television viewers around the world in handling the live coverage of the miners' emergence to safety. I've written books and delivered speeches from places in my heart every

Thomas Baldrick, the only live TV reporter on the scene for the miraculous rescue of "The QueCreek Nine."

bit as deep as a coalmine. I've flown upside down in an open cockpit T-6 airplane. I've done a Native American Vision Quest, and studied at a hands-on healing school.

I've even climbed a telephone pole (called the "Pamper Pole" for good reason) and managed to guide myself to stand on the tiny area on top of it as my legs trembled more than I ever knew they could. If you've ever looked at a telephone pole, you'll realize there is nothing to hold onto at the peak. A person must manage to get one foot planted on top for leverage to push the rest of their body into a standing position without losing their balance.

While I was wearing a harness for safety, I certainly couldn't remember it. A harness in that situation does nothing to calm one's fear. Wearing a pair of cowboy boots at the time made a terrifying scenario even more difficult for me.

Experience has proven to me that living with courage is living fully. But first, I must first admit to having fear. Next, I have to get it out of my face so I can look at the situation that is scaring me. Only then, is it possible for me to find choices and a viable solution. I realize courage and fear go hand in hand. Therein lies the answer!

I visualize holding my courage in one hand and my fear in the other. Since I will always have both, I need to learn how to balance the two. Now, whenever my fear comes up, I can admit it and recognize it. I can choose to hold my fear in my hand, continue to focus on it, and give it the power to stop me.

Another choice for me is to say, "Oh, I know you. You're just fear. That's all you are. It's normal that you're here. In fact, I should have been expecting you." Then, I can choose to look at my other hand where my courage is waiting patiently to be called upon once again for active duty. I can ask my courage to help me see, and help me get to where I want to be. It does work.

The solution is not to overcome your fear. I believe it is more about owning it, and placing it at arm's length. In doing so, you will find the power to focus on your courage, and embrace it as your choice.

TIME. I saved this life lesson from the miners for last, as I do with audiences during speeches. Time is a challenge that hits home for all of us. Therefore, a lesson that directly touches an issue for us and sheds light on it can be quite powerful.

Are you one of those people who is short on time? Do you have enough of it? Are you always looking for time? If this is you, let me take the time to fill you in on a little secret. You will only find time when you make it. Talk to my raised hand with your excuses: "Oh, but you don't understand. I have this to do. I have that to do. Then I have to go here. Then I have to go there. Blah, blah, blah, blah, blah." Stop.

The next time you want to complain about not having enough time, remember the name Dennis J. Hall. He was the seventh of the QueCreek Nine to be lifted safely to the rest of his life. Ironically, the 49-year old hails from Johnstown, PA, the home of the famous flood in 1889. Dennis was the one, who as 50 million gallons of water was converging on him, made a call to another mining team of nine to say, "Get out! We've hit water! Get the hell out! Go!" (In later interviews, when asked why he did it, Dennis Hall answered, "I had to. I had to.")

Because that team escaped before the unleashed water reached them, the rescue effort was named "Nine for Nine." That those first nine miners lived, they were able to keep alive one of the greatest modern-day examples of time management. If Dennis Hall took the time to make a life-saving call when his own life was on the line, we all have the time to do the big and little things we want to do, and need to do in our lives.

For the sake of this book, I'll bring it home again. We all have time to celebrate a child. Recently, I heard John Phillippi, the fifth miner to escape with his life, as he shared insights he has learned about time. The man the miners called "Flathead," seems to be pretty well-rounded in his perspective. He spoke of living life in the moment, and not taking any moment for granted because of never knowing when they can be taken away. He gave an example of how he knows better to have a catch when his 12-year old son asks. He says he shouldn't offer the boy to wait until tomorrow night because you never know if tomorrow is going to come.

Try to consider these lessons from the miners as you live fully in moments of celebrating the child in you or a child in your life.

The Wall Of Hope

Most walls are built for the purpose of separation. The Wall of Hope was built to bring people together. It stands tall as a snapshot of what American children were feeling at the time of the first anniversary of the 9-11 tragedies. Before I get into more details of it, I must first lay the foundation for you on which the Wall was built.

I committed myself to the wall project early on the evening of July 28, 2002. I was alone with my thoughts, heading eastbound on the Pennsylvania Turnpike from Somerset to Harrisburg, the state capital.

Staying below the speed limit, my goal was to avoid an encounter with the police. I didn't want a roadside sobriety check to detect the level of Mountain Dew I had in my bloodstream to keep me going!

I was "Doing the Dew" having pulled an "all-nighter" doing the live TV coverage of the miner's rescue the night before. Yes, I was tired but equally wired from the adrenaline rush of being an eyewitness to the magical ending. I was looking forward to a couple of hours of sleep, because the next morning I knew I'd be waking up with the roosters, having booked Governor Schweiker for a live interview on ABC's "Good Morning America." On the drive, I was also thinking about the past few days of working closely with the Governor and members of his staff. Based on seeing what caring people they were, I had every reason to believe they would stand behind my idea for a 9-11 Wall of Hope.

I remember realizing during that drive, how I had not only been a witness to history, but played a small role in it, too. It was a nice feeling to have, because recent history was a subject I was struggling with at the time as a television journalist.

Students at Shanksville-Stonycreek Elementary view "The Wall of Hope."
Photo by Rusty Kennedy.

Thomas Baldrick stands at the first finished piece of the wall built with love.
Who cares that he can't hammer a nail straight or doesn't even own a toolbox?

I openly discuss details of my emotional trauma related to 9-11. Though some may perceive it as weakness, I hope my being vocal about it may help someone else who still remembers, to realize they are not alone. Publicly I admit how I long for the day when I don't think of 9-11 or touch the pain I carry from it. Surprisingly, this does not embarrass me. I accept it as my truth. What I saw, what I heard, what I felt, and what I learned while covering the story for ABC News in New York and Shanksville seems as though it has changed me forever.

While many Americans have moved on or grown bored with the 9-11 issue, I cannot forget. Whenever I am asked to talk about those tragic events, I feel a baseball-sized lump in my throat. I know then, it is only a matter of time before more tears emerge from a place inside of me that surely I thought would have run dry by now.

Since I worked straight through the night of September 11, 2001, the first of my heinous nightmares related to the tragedies came during the early morning hours of September 13th. They continued to sneak into my bedroom night after night after night for more than six weeks. Mostly, they centered on a theme of me watching helplessly as people were killed in painful and awful ways. The nightmares were so bad, I fell into a constant battle with fatigue. I was just too afraid to go to sleep willingly.

Finally, on Saturday morning, November 3, 2001, came the first time I was able to save a life in my nightmares. Only in the dream, it cost me mine. I vividly recall the speeding black SUV as it prepared to run down a toddler-sized boy. I ran in and was able to lift the little guy from harm's way, but for some reason I stood and faced the vehicle as it hit me head on, sending me flying into the air. The impact of the collision was so real and so brutally violent, that I awoke from my sleep standing upright at the foot of my bed.

All morning, I cried through moments of despair, frustration, confusion, and fear. I decided come Monday, I was going to seek professional help. In a merciful piece of irony, it was no longer necessary because that granddaddy of them all wound up marking the real-life death of my post 9-11 nightmares.

When Al Queda's evil hit our homeland, my first book, *KIDS RULE! The Hopes and Dreams of 21st Century Children* was just completed, but not yet released. Therefore, no members of the media were calling me to do interviews for their shows or articles like they do today. No one knew or cared if I had opinions or ways to help children deal with their trauma caused by the events of 9-11.

It was tough for me being unable to speak out as adults across our nation were glued to their TV sets, almost hypnotized by coverage of the story. I knew millions of children would also be upset by the events, especially the images of planes crashing into buildings. My guess was the worst part for a child came from sensing the fear and sadness of their mommy, daddy, and other grownups. I know children feed off those emotions and it was a bitter pill to swallow.

Another upsetting thing for me was the immediate backlash and insatiable craving to "Bomb Afghanistan back to the Stone Age." Surely, the message we teach children about conflict resolution was not "Shoot and ask questions later." Hearing the claims of some experts interviewed in the media that children would not be impacted by all of this because "Words are just words," made me wonder if in fact the Stone Age was returning to America on the way to Afghanistan.

For the aforementioned reasons, I decided to build The Wall of Hope in time for the first anniversary of 9-11. My own hopes of healing were attached to the outcome.

I hoped to give children an outlet to express themselves and feel good for doing it. I hoped the attention surrounding the Wall would help adults to take a closer look into the hearts and heads of children. Many kids remain scared. I know many adults feel the same way.

9-11 is a difficult subject to discuss, and even more difficult to understand. Nonetheless, I hoped the wall could open much-needed channels of communication between my scared fellow Americans, young and old. Finally, I hoped it would create some peace in my own heart about 9-11 where before there was only pain.

The Children of 9-11 Wall of Hope is a 50-foot wide collage of the thoughts, feelings, fears, observations, poems, prayers and drawings of children across Pennsylvania. Many of the children who contributed to the Wall were directly affected by the losses from Flight 93 and the World Trade Center.

I had the honor of working with young ones from the families of the heroes onboard Flight 93. I was also blessed to connect with the students from Shanksville, whose school was within a mile or two of where the plane crashed. Children from Royersford Elementary, the Feltonville-Horn School, St. William, Anne Frank, and the Dobson School also shared signs of how special they are.

There were many more human bricks that formed The Wall of Hope. My cousin, Stephen Druding, helped me to design it. Abel Ubinas, a friend I didn't know I had, built the structures for it. Sharla Feldscher, my friend and publicist, Rosemarie Tipton, Principal of the Shanksville-Stonycreek Elementary School, Karen Model of NOVA (the Network of Victim Assistance), and

Maria McClatchey embracing her Poems of Remembrance. She is proud to know what the author didn't … the difference between a limerick, a haiku, and an acroustic poem!

Smiles in Shanksville are great symbols of hope.

A big group of kids in Shanksville including Thomas and Governor Mark Schweiker.

David LaTorre, Press Secretary for Governor Schweiker were the cement that held the wall together.

On the morning of September 11, 2002, The Children of 9-11 Wall of Hope was unveiled. Shortly before we attended the memorial service at the Flight 93 crash site, Pennsylvania Governor Schweiker was at my side as we joined the entire family of Shanksville-Stonycreek Elementary.

It was a powerful and precious moment in time for all who were there. The fun and connection that these small-town little ones had with their Governor and me is a celebration I'll still be cherishing when their kids are attending school in Shanksville.

The Governor later mentioned the Wall in his speech at the Flight 93 Memorial Service. He also used it as the cornerstone of his televised speech that night from the state capital.

It is currently the hope of the Families of Flight 93, and many others across Pennsylvania that my Children of 9-11 Wall of Hope will be on permanent display when the official National Historic Landmark Memorial of United Airlines Flight 93 is created in Shanksville. Who am I to argue with such brilliance and wisdom? I too believe it is the perfect open home for sharing with the world.

I have done some touring with the wall as a way to raise money and awareness for the Flight 93 Memorial. Somehow, I hope everyone gets a chance to see it. I've joked that if The Children of 9-11 Wall of Hope doesn't touch a person in some way, they'd best be dialing 9-1-1 to call for an ambulance because something must be wrong with their heart!

The following pages are samples of the priceless pieces of work created for The Children of 9-11 Wall of Hope. I have also included samples of the rewards that come naturally if you celebrate a child by listening to his or her voice.

Dean Jones - Philadelphia, PA
Age 14
I hope that we can get along with everyone in this world. Learn to love each other.

I hope that the victims families are okay.

Andrew
Age 9

When God brings you to it. God brings you through it.

Kathryn Felt
9-10-02

If I don't think
about it
I don't
Remember It!

9-11-01

Our harts are broken

GREAT WAS YOUR SACRIFICE

LORRAINE Bay
SANDRA BRADSHAW
JASON DAHL
WANDA GREEN
LEROY HOMER
CEE LYLES
DEBORAH WELSH
CHRISTIAN ADAMS
TODD BEAMER
ALAN BEAVEN
MARK BINGHAM
DEORA BODLEY
MARION BRITTON
THOMAS E. BURNETT JR.
WILLIAM CASHMAN
JOSEPH DELUCA
PATRICK DRISCOLL
EDWARD FELT
PATRICIA CUSHING
COLLEEN FRASER
ANDREW GARCIA
JEREMY GLICK
KRISTEN GOULD
LAUREN GRANDCOLAS
DONALD F. GREENE
LINDA GRONLUND
RICHARD GUADAGNO
JOSHUA KUGE
HILDA MARCIN
NICOLE MILLER
LOUIS J. NACKE
MARK ROTHENBURG
CHRISTINE SNYDER
JOHN TELIGNANT
HONOR WAINIO
JANE C. FOLGER
DONALD PETERSON
JEAN PETERSON
GEORGINE CORRIGAN
WALESKA MARTINEZ

FLIGHT   93

Maria McClatchey
Grade 3

There once was a town called
Shanksville
Where life was Peaceful and Tranquil
Then in came a Plane
That crashed on the Lane
And disturbed the qUiet of
Shanksville

Limerick

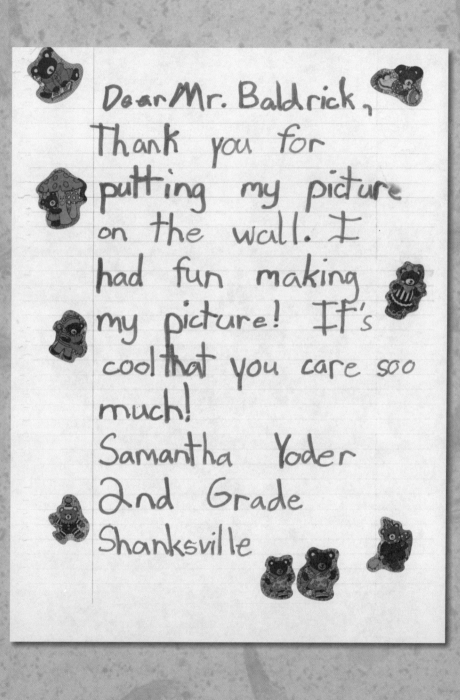

Dear Mr. Baldrick,
Thank you for
putting my picture
on the wall. I
had fun making
my picture! It's
cool that you care soo
much!
Samantha Yoder
2nd Grade
Shanksville

Totally cool

Handsome

Outstanding

Majorly Funky

Awesome

Superman!

Maria M.

Dear Mr. Baldrick

Thank you for honoring me, and placing my prayer on The Wall of Hope. It was a priviledge in meeting you, and the Governor. I appreciate the time you took in the Wall of Hope. Once again thankyou and may God Bless America.

Sincerly,
Sam Shober

Dear Mr. Baldrick   9/02
God remembers people
who share with others,
thanks you for being one of
those people and for sharing
with me and the kids at
Shanksville.

Love,
Bridget Statzman

Dear Mr. Baldrick

Thank you for coming to our school. Thank you for making the wall of hope. It was very nice to meet you.

your friend
Katie Foy   3rd grade

Shanksville Stonycreek School

Just Because

Play charades with a child.

Cuddle and take a nap with a child.

Make imprints of a child's precious little hands.

Offer a child a helping hand whenever they need it.

Watch and listen to a child sleep.

Get a child a Teddy Bear.

Tickle a child.

Let a child tickle you.

Flash a child a "just because" smile.

Treat a child to surprise early "pick-ups" at school.

Turn a child on to Frank Sinatra like my Aunt Mary did for me.

Wrap gifts for a child.

Get balloons for a child.

Leave love notes in a child's school lunch.

Hide surprises for a child.

Support a child's hobbies.

Share your hobbies with a child.

Suggest more suitable behaviors when a child acts out.

Be comfortable with a child exploring their body.

Give comfort when a child is afraid.

Present a child with reasons and options.

Say "yes" whenever you can.

So Well Done, It's Rare

"I base my classroom on the golden rule. The most important thing we can teach children is how to treat each other. They need so many skills to be a survivor in this world. Academics won't mean much if kids can't enjoy each other and feel for each other. How we treat kids is far more important than what we say to them."

—MRS. DUNN, *first grade teacher,*
Shanksville-Stonycreek Elementary

In the true sense of the word "unbelievable," this story surely qualifies. The last piece to it contains the kind of details you're likely going to want to share with others. It involves an astonishing celebration of children on 9-11 by a woman whose personal world was rocked by two of the three plane crashes that day.

Along the way to the ending, you'll learn how truly spectacular a simple, caring woman can be. You'll see a small-town teacher can indeed make a world of difference. You'll discover an "old school" approach and a good, old-fashioned work ethic can pave the way for the future even in the 21st Century. You'll learn these things because Joyce Dunn is a teacher, and an unbelievable one at that.

The lessons are simple and simply timeless. Joyce Dunn, the teacher and the woman, understands that even in a complex world, children still need the basics . . . the ABC's of reading and being good to one another.

Her job as a first-grade teacher is so well done that it's rare. This sentiment resounds again and again from the students, parents, and career educators who know Joyce Dunn. Seemingly, she is in a class by herself. Her principal, Rosemarie Tipton, readily admits, "There are very few like Joyce Dunn in teaching."

Joyce Dunn touches the future as a teacher.

Joyce is now an overnight sensation as a teacher—after 34-years in the making! As of late, she has received distinguished honors, including the 2003 Pennsylvania Teacher of the Year Award. At the award finals, a little angel named Maria McClatchey, whom she taught in first grade, nominated Joyce. Here is an excerpt of Maria's speech:

> "We kind of live in the middle of nowhere. But now the whole world knows about us because of Flight 93 and the nine trapped miners. I'm told that miracles come in three's. I think our next miracle should be Mrs. Dunn winning Teacher of the Year. Not that she needs a miracle to win.
>
> One of the great things about Mrs. Dunn is that she lets all of the kids learn at their own pace and no one feels different or left out because of how fast or slow they learn. Mrs. Dunn teaches reading, math, respect, love, kindness, and hope. She plants seeds of love in everyone's heart and treats everyone with respect. She loves all the kids in her classroom no matter how they behave.
>
> I think Mrs. Dunn should be Teacher of the Year because she is so full of love and because she gives the best squishy hugs, especially for somebody so thin. Love is what creates miracles. Thanks to Mrs. Dunn, students at Shanksville are surrounded by miracles every day. Not the big ones that everyone hears about on the news, but more importantly, the little ones that affect us children for life."

After receiving the award, Joyce joked it was in the swimsuit competition where she won over the judges. But seriously she said, "Winning Teacher of the Year was a really humbling experience, but not the highlight of my career. Every spring, when a child takes off and starts to become an independent reader and you see that glow in their eyes and they say, 'Mrs. Dunn! I can read!' There isn't any award in the world that can touch that."

Joyce loves schoolteachers so much she married one. Her husband, Charles, later became a school superintendent. He is now a minister. On the other hand, the only career switch Joyce ever made, was taking years off from teaching to stay at home with each of their four baby boys.

Beginning as a teacher in 1960, Joyce has spent 27 years in a classroom in rural Somerset County, PA. School Superintendent Gary A. Singel has known Joyce throughout her Shanksville career. He recalls, "Early on, the Dunn family moved to Virginia. Then, about two years later, they returned. Joyce was looking for a teaching job and it just so happened we had an opening. I thought, 'Why would I want anybody else when I can have Joyce?' The greatest compliment I could give anybody who leaves a job is to rehire them. We took Joyce back right away."

No matter where she's taught, no matter when, Joyce says two things in the classroom have never changed. "I can remember from the first day I taught," she said. "The hearts of the teachers and the hearts of the kids are still the same. What happens between those two is what creates the magic in the classroom we call learning."

Joyce Dunn knows a lot about learning. She is also a magician who uses love and dedication over slight of hand. And, just like any good magic trick, learning the contents of Joyce Dunn's personal report card will have you wondering, "How does she do that?"

SUBJECT: History. GRADE: A+

History repeating itself is often not a good thing. Though in this case it clearly was, thanks to a specific experience involving a history teacher with big red curly hair and big blue eyes. Her name was Ms. Hewitt, and she taught Joyce Dunn in the seventh grade.

Growing up in Altoona, PA, Joyce's father, like many others worked on the railroad. Not long before she was to attend seventh grade, Joyce's father suffered a stroke. The Dunn family had no hospitalization, and no income with him out of work.

The problems at home were only part of what derailed young Joyce. She had an extremely difficult transition into junior high school. She recalls, "Everybody got new clothes, but we had no money. I was just trying to fade into the background because I felt so inferior." The feelings ran deeper than her wardrobe. They affected her confidence and education. Until one day, Ms. Hewitt brought it all to a grinding halt.

"She gave us a project to do," said Joyce. "Kids were doing elaborate presentations. They were impressive, and kids had clearly spent money on them. Yet I had to make mine out of things around the house.

When the day came for me to show my project, I was so embarrassed. I made a little scene of dolls in colonial clothes. It looked pretty drab. Near the end of my presentation in front of the class, I was just about to break down and cry. But Ms. Hewitt came over, put her arm around me, and began to explain all of the wonderful things she saw in my project. Immediately, my peers changed their attitude and began to see my project through Ms. Hewitt's eyes. Kids actually applauded.

My self-esteem turned around right then and there. Her sensitivity helped me so much, I said to myself, 'I can be somebody. I want to be like Ms. Hewitt. I want to make other kids feel like she made me feel.' Ever since then, I can't remember a time when I didn't want to teach."

SUBJECT: Conduct. GRADE: A+

Superintendent Singel often sings Joyce's praises. "What makes her so special is her true sincerity and passion. That is not something you can teach. You're either born with the ability to nurture, educate, and reach others, or you're not. Kids view her as family, almost like a grandmother. I have never seen anybody in all my years that has such patience with young children. Even on days when she's not feeling well, the car is not working, or something personal has upset her, Joyce is amazingly caring and patient with her children. She is always nurturing, even to me."

Ms. Tipton believes a great sense of humor helps Joyce be patient. "She always says 'Mrs. Dunn.' She never says 'I.' The kids just know she cares and is watching. It's not that she has incredible classroom control. You don't always see her kids sitting quietly.

I've literally seen them climbing the walls, but she never, ever yells. She'll just get them down, put them back in their seats, and try the lesson all over again."

Mrs. Dunn describes her goal this way: "To provide an environment where children can be themselves, and not be ridiculed or put down. I want my class to be a place where kids can grow and feel like everything is going to be okay." She remembers to let her students be little kids.

Joyce adds, "There must be some place in a child's life where they can be safe. There was a time when that place was home. Sadly enough, it's not always the case anymore. Often there aren't adults at home. A lot of kids have to fend for themselves. I have little six-year olds who come in with their shirt on backwards, a price tag on their clothes, or their hair completely uncombed. I talk with them and find out that the adults in the home were gone. Imagine, a six-year old having to wake up, get dressed, have breakfast, and make it to the school bus all on their own."

Some years ago, there was a little girl who had recently moved into the district. A month or so later, she went home after school one day and nobody was there. The police were called and came to help the scared six-year old. They asked the girl where her parents were. She didn't know. They asked her how to contact them. She didn't know that either. When police asked her whom they should call, the girl answered excitedly, "Call my teacher, Mrs. Dunn! She'll know what to do!"

Sure enough, police followed the girl's advice. Joyce knew the parents were divorced and had the telephone number of the father. She said, "Apparently, the mother just forgot to come home. It's sad, but true."

After only a month with one child, you could say, well done, Mrs. Dunn!

SUBJECT: Getting Results. GRADE: A+

"You can't get better than Joyce," claims Principal Rosemarie Tipton. "Her scores in the national tests have always been in the 90 percentile. This means more than ninety-percent of the first-grade classes in the country do worse than hers. And it happens every single year."

So, how does she do it? Joyce explains, "I use a multi-sensory approach in as many things as I can. Some kids are visual. Some are auditory or kinesthetic. I never just assume a child learned a concept. I don't just lecture either. I find a number of different ways to re-teach lessons."

Ms. Tipton points out, "Joyce doesn't kill time with videos or allow interruptions. She spends 80% of the time on reading and 20% on math. All other subjects fall under those two areas. She gets the job done by continuous time on task. She's like a plow horse, not a racehorse."

"I've taught kindergarten and second grade, too. But there is something special about first grade," says Joyce. "You have the excitement of watching them become readers." She knows first grade leaves a first and lasting impression on children. "Research shows if a kid has a bad first-grade experience, they will likely remain negative on education. Early literacy can trickle through to eliminate many problems like truancy and violence. It's usually poor readers who act out in all these other ways. If they can't read after first grade, the doors to them get shut. It's not about a child's intelligence if they can't read and write."

Leaders are limited to those who can get others to follow. "I tell my parents I expect kids to read on grade level and that I need their help," says Joyce. "Parent helpers are such a powerful resource. I have at least one in my room at all times. Moms and dads arrange their schedules to be in class. It's so addictive for them. They understand so much better what their child is going through, and see how a teacher relates to discipline or learning problems. There's not too many who don't want to be a good parent. They just don't have the skills, especially if it's a first child. I make it my responsibility to show parents skills they can use."

I can hear it now. You're thinking, *I don't know of too many classrooms where parents help on a daily basis. It's tough enough to get a good turnout for a Parent-Teacher Night.* I agree. Let Mr. Singel explain. "It's almost like Joyce handles parents with kid gloves as she does with the children. She never chastises them. She always finds something good to say, but they'll get her message about what's right and what's not. I'm still not sure how she does it, but Joyce is one of those rare people who cannot only tell you where you're going to go, she'll convince you wholeheartedly that you're going to enjoy the trip!"

SUBJECT: Homework. GRADE: A+

Surprise! Joyce Dunn doesn't give much homework. "During the day we have a lot of time on task," she says. They really work hard during the day. That's enough. They're only six years old."

Such recognition alone makes Joyce award-worthy in my book. I don't like how we're creating little hunchbacked kids because of their daily burden of carrying book bags that seem to weigh as much as they do. Also, the more competitive grownups make learning, the more it can become an emotional burden for little ones.

Joyce reasons, "Most kids come through daycare. By first grade, many are already under such pressure that they have emotional baggage at six years old." Is it any wonder we think kids grow up so quickly today?

Joyce adds, "During open house the first week of school, I tell parents how the children work so hard during the day, they need time to play, outside if possible. They need time to have fun, and in the summer, too. Kids need to do kid things like running, playing, and daydreaming."

SUBJECT: Extra Credit. GRADE: A+

Joyce Dunn is one of those teachers who makes going beyond the call of duty, the call of duty. School superintendent Singel has seen it all from her. "I can remember a number of occasions when a child was waiting to be picked up after school, but the parent never showed. Joyce would calmly attempt to find the parent, while the child was angry, frustrated, and embarrassed. Eventually, Joyce would say to the child, 'I'll tell you what, why don't you come home with me?' Even if it was not one of her students or if the child lived on the other side of the district, she would take the child home, feed them dinner, and make them feel good. Once she reached the parents later, Joyce would drive the child home. She didn't even make the parents pick up their own kid! She just has no qualms about tending to children beyond the expected role of teachers."

There's more—Joyce privately tutors her own students. She says, "If I have someone that needs extra help and there isn't enough time during class, I'll ask the parents if they could pick up the child after school, about 4:30. After all the other children are gone and the building is so quiet, you can get so much accomplished and develop such a strong rapport with a child. When I get them to reading at grade level, I stop. It's just a small thing a teacher can do."

But, Mrs. Dunn is never done with her small things. "I often tutor in the summer, too," she says. I don't ever take any money for that. I think it's part of my job as a teacher to give that extra help." Principal Tipton says it goes beyond that. "Every month, Joyce sends children a summer packet. Until the day they start second grade, they're her kids."

Somehow, there's even more. We turn again to Ms. Tipton. "Joyce has so many dimensions. She visits nursing homes. She is active in her church. People always share things in confidence with her. She's a neat lady. As a teacher, she sometimes writes letters to parents. If they don't respond, she will intrude into their lives to let them know that there is someone else who cares."

You'll never guess how Joyce the magician does this trick. She follows a school bus to a child's home! "I often do that just to get an idea of their background, especially if I have a bad feeling about a child. Very often the quiet kids have the biggest burdens. Most nights I drive my husband crazy because I can't get to sleep without thinking about at least one child. 'What's going on with them? What can I do? Why were they so quiet today?' Too many children have such big chips on their shoulder for being only six-years old. They are so fragile at that age so I just try my best to make those chips melt away."

SUBJECT: September 11, 2001. GRADE: A-mazing!

Though it may be hard to believe, this final subject on my report card for Joyce Dunn is true. If for some reason, you don't think it celebrates children, please consult your doctor. This is truly a tale to remember.

The news of the World Trade Center being hit by airplanes spread quickly through the Shanksville-Stonycreek Elementary School. Minutes after the first plane crash, another teacher told Joyce what happened. But good ol' Mrs. Dunn simply closed her door and said nothing to the students. Unlike many teachers across the country, she did not turn on a TV in her classroom.

Joyce Dunn kept right on teaching her first graders. "I had a sickening feeling," she said. "I just turned Michael over to God." The Michael referred to was Joyce's 32-year old son. Michael Dunn worked for the Sperry Rail Service, using computers to check the subway system in New York City. Michael worked under Tower 1 of the World Trade Center.

"No. I didn't say anything at school," Joyce said. I just had an overwhelming feeling to make the children feel calm. A few minutes later, the school shook. We heard a boom or a crashing sound. We could see smoke through the windows. The building truly shook. All of the kids got silent. They asked, 'What happened, Mrs. Dunn?' I told them, 'We don't know, but we'll find out.' Parents were anxious and started to come into school to take their kids home. We didn't dismiss early because we didn't know what was going on. We thought we should keep the children where they were." Mrs. Dunn kept right on teaching.

Principal Rosemarie Tipton adds, "It was an orderly day. Everyone on the staff played it very cool. No children were upset unless parents came in upset. I didn't even know about Joyce's son until the end of the day."

Joyce said, "Later, when we found out that Flight 93 had gone down just over the hill, we told the children a plane had crashed, but that their families were all right. Kids lived nearby and we didn't want them worried about their house being hit."

The 9-11 tragedies in New York and Shanksville came eerily close to home for Joyce Dunn. I cannot imagine how she kept herself together that day, knowing United Airlines Flight 93 had just missed crashing into her classroom, AND terrorists had toppled the World Trade Center where her son worked.

Joyce explained it this way: "If you had 24 little pairs of eyes watching you and they were all very vulnerable and would become frightened or hysterical, you would have called upon yourself to be calm and reassuring. They were depending on me for their safety. They were relying on me thinking, 'If Mrs. Dunn is not upset, then it's going to be okay.'"

Nitsa McClatchey was working as a parent volunteer for Mrs. Dunn on September 11th. "When I walked into the first-grade classroom at 2:00 p.m., she was teaching a lesson on vowel sounds. Then, the telephone rang. Mrs. Dunn answered the call, sighed deeply, and simply said, 'Thank you.' I asked her if everything was all right. She said, 'Michael is fine.' I asked, 'Michael, your son?' She said, 'Yes. He works at the World Trade Center.' I asked her how she had made it through the day without knowing how he was. She said, 'Prayer.' She then continued to teach the lesson on vowel sounds! I went out into the hall and cried."

(Joyce's husband, Charles, called the school after he reached Michael on his cell phone. It was Kimberly in the school's front office that informed Joyce. It turns out that Michael Dunn was crossing the George Washington Bridge when the first tower was hit. Since he worked late the night before, he was told to come into work late in the morning.)

The final celebration of children I will now share about Joyce Dunn gives me the same thrill I've enjoyed many times as a journalist. It's called "getting a scoop." At the time of this writing, everyone in the Shanksville-Stonycreek School District believes Joyce Dunn is retiring at the end of the current school year. She is not. "I think I'd really miss it," she admits. "I think I'll just keep showing up. I touch the future. I am a teacher."

Heads Of The Class

When I do school assemblies, or speak to groups of parents or educators, I always tell audiences how I've grown to feel about teachers. I am proud to be "pro-teacher" despite knowing they have so many critics. If only a fraction of the critics tried the job themselves, the shortage of teachers would be ended faster than you could say "detention." The critics would also quickly learn the trials and tribulations of modern-day teaching.

Most career teachers truly want to help children to learn and grow. They aren't getting rich, but they should be. After all, if you think about it, many teachers today are more than educators. They have multiple jobs that make them a hybrid of childhood helpers: caretakers, family counselors, psychologists, police officers, fortune-tellers, etc.

Since many kids today aren't getting their needs met at home, teachers have their work cut out for them even more. They often have too many students and not enough time with them in order to guarantee that we raise the bar in education while leaving no child behind. As you just read, even consummate professionals like Joyce Dunn can't do it all on their own. Teachers must have the support of parents.

When I was a kid, I wish someone had explained to me that teachers are human beings. It may sound funny, but I'm being serious. I never realized teachers had personal lives outside of school. I never thought family concerns, financial woes, or relationship problems affected them.

I didn't know anything about the pressure and responsibility they had, or the obstacles and limitations that stood in their way.

I was just a typical kid who often saw teachers simply as authority figures. I wanted to learn how they worked and how much

I could get away with in their class. For me, school was fairly easy. The real challenge was to discover new ways to have fun.

I used to be proud about being the all-time demerit champion at my high school. It's ironic that I now have many educators as friends. I suppose since I can't do anything to change the past, the best I can do now is try to prevent other kids from being like me. I know if we celebrate teachers, we will also be helping and celebrating children.

Heads Of The Class

Stay in close contact with a child's teachers.

Volunteer to be a teacher's helper.

Join a school's Parent-Teacher Association.

Explain to a child how teachers are human.

Share your school experiences with a child.

Share helpful personal information regarding a child with their teachers.

Give your contact information to a child's teachers.

Use proper grammar around the house.

Don't overload a child with extracurricular activities.

Give rewards for solid report cards.

Support school plays and shows.

Support school athletic events.

Be a school dance chaperone.

Get a child into the habit of eating a healthy breakfast.

Check out the school cafeteria lunches.

Get to know a child's school nurse.

Get to know a child's school bus driver.

Get to know a child's school administrators.

Get a child into a comfortable after-school routine.

Make sure a child isn't upset before heading off to school.

How To Give A Child The Best School Year Ever

As another school year was approaching, I was contacted by a number of representatives from media outlets who were interested in interviewing me. They wanted to know if I had any advice or tips to share for dealing successfully with children. Being a big kid myself, doing a great deal of work with children, and being a grownup who kids often feel safe enough with to tell everything, I suppose this combination does provide for quite an interesting perspective.

I wrote something for newspaper and broadcasting reporters titled, "How to Give a Child the Best School Year Ever." Since I don't feel it is my right to tell people what to do, I kept consistent with my preference to merely make suggestions and observations for others to consider.

The work was so well-received by columnists like Sally Friedman of the Burlington County Times in New Jersey, I decided it might be nice to include in this book. I hope you receive it as fertile ground for finding ways to celebrate a child.

Imagine our world if we all had most of the summer off from work! For many of us, it wouldn't be fun or easy to jump right back into our jobs and produce peak performances. It would require change. We might be bored. We might be tired. Some of us might even be cranky.

Why then, do we often fail to see that children have quite an adjustment returning to school? Don't forget, their potential stress of trying to fit in and learn with new kids and teachers, too. Perhaps, now you'll see how both you and your child can get off to a better start and have a more enjoyable school year, *if YOU* do *YOUR* homework, too!

■ Listen with Your Heart

Be loving and patient when talking with a child. Take a moment to ask about their day (when you're not multi-tasking!) Listen to what they're saying, and what they're *not* saying, so you can really understand.

Don't yell if you don't like the news. Yelling will only discourage a child from sharing with you. There will be many times when you'll wish you had open communication with your kids. Otherwise, when they do get in trouble, you'll angrily ask them, "Why didn't you tell me about this?" *I'm telling you why right now!*

Trust your child. If you make it safe for them to tell you the truth, they will. If they say there's a serious problem at school, don't write it off.

■ Study History – Don't Live It!

The past is history—the future a mystery—the only school work that matters is the assignment they're doing in the present. Each school day and each school year is a fresh start. If a child was a struggling "C" student in fourth grade, be positive about fifth grade and help them to be positive, too. Improving to grades of B's and A's is entirely possible. On the flip side, remind your child that last year's A's aren't IRA's. They don't roll over from year to year.

■ 2 + 1 = A

Two parents helping one child—that's how kids learn best. It gives them the best chance to get A's. Own your share of responsibility for your child's education. Single parents may want to consider the child's teacher as the second person. Keep in close contact with teachers and know what you can do to help them with your child.

■ Teach your children about Teachers

One doesn't enter this profession to get rich or to have summers off. Most teachers work many hours and put hundreds of their own dollars into their classroom every year. Teachers choose this career because they care. Humanize them. If you and your child see a teacher as a person with their own life and their own issues to deal with, you'll all enjoy a better relationship.

Also, realize that teachers are under tremendous pressure and have their hands tied more than you know. The U.S. Government's agenda to "raise the bar, but leave no child behind" has raised expectations of teachers to deliver higher test scores. Meanwhile, this is to happen without raising teacher salaries, morale, or their level of resources and support.

Teach a child that respect, appreciation, and their best effort to learn, taste much sweeter to teachers than apples.

■ Show and Tell: Don't Assume

A student's school day should begin with a healthy start. Make them eat a good breakfast and feed their little souls every morning, too. Show kids you love them. Tell kids you love them. It stays with them throughout their day and may make a world of difference when their world gets tough.

■ Remember the Kid Inside of You

Treat your kids the way *you* wished you were treated! Be supportive. Provide structure. Enjoy them every chance you can. They grow up fast!

■ Tell Me Something You Learned Today

If you want dialogue with your child, ask questions they can answer. Don't just ask, "How was your day?" You're going to hear, "Okay." Instead, try this one. "What was the best moment you had today?" (It will encourage children to think positive.) Or, "Tell me one thing you learned today." (Your child will know they must remember at least one thing to tell you.)

Over the course of a week, that's five lessons learned. Over a month, it's 20. Over a school year, it's a total of 180. Not bad! You may even learn a few extra lessons yourself!

Ready To Read, Ready To Learn

I love Laura Bush. As a former teacher and librarian, the First Lady has made early literacy a top priority. The timing is right for her "Ready to Read, Ready to Learn" initiative.

While her husband focused on Saddam Hussein's "weapons of mass destruction in Iraq," Laura Bush defended our country in another important battle. In her case, we have no one but ourselves to blame for the weapon of mass destruction involved. I call this self-inflicted crisis, "The Dumbing Down of America."

Since we do enjoy freedom in our country, we can do whatever we want within the confines of the law. We can watch TV, surf the net, or play games all day long. We can choose to stop stretching our minds through proven activities such as reading. Each of us is free to stunt our intellectual growth, and quiet our quest for higher knowledge.

Freedom of speech means we can say what we want. However, for the sake of our children, can we please make an attempt to sound more intelligent? I can no longer accept daily doses of "I seen that movie." Nor can I spend another day hearing, "He don't got no money."

Exercising these freedoms that impede our education and intelligence, is anything but free. In fact, when adults make these poor choices, they come at a hefty price. Unfortunately, the ones who pay severely are our children.

Mrs. Bush believes "Children who are read to learn two things: one, that reading is worthwhile, and two, that they are worthwhile." Reading with a child shows them you want them to learn. It is also time well spent because it bonds you with a child and shows them that you care.

I'm thrilled how the NBA acts like a champion with their high profile program, "Read to Achieve." I'm sure it has made a difference in the life of a child. I try to do the same. In my appearances at schools, I make kids laugh with a funny face that shows what they look like watching television. Coming from a TV career, I hope children listen when I tell them that watching TV is *not* going to help them to live their hopes and dreams. However, reading will.

Reading activates a child's creativity and imagination. It opens their world to new words, new interests, and new ideas. Good readers make good writers and good speakers. Children with those skills present a better image with others. They are often more confident, more likeable, and have a higher sense of self-esteem. To put it in a young person's terms, "Reading Rocks!" So rock on, grownups! Read with a child!

I give the First Lady an "A" for her efforts in promoting literacy. She is our nation's teacher and is helping to make our children and our nation stronger. She says, "All parents and children can experience the magic and joy of reading together. This is the foundation for success in school—and in life." I couldn't agree more.

Ready To Read, Ready To Learn

Here are some ways you can celebrate a child through reading:

Share time at a bookstore.

Share time at a library.

Get a child a library card.

Attend appearances by authors.

Give books as presents.

Write your own stories with a child.

Do a crossword puzzle with a child.

Create a family cookbook.

Attend book discussion group meetings with a child.

Stress the importance of reading.

Look into (RIF) Reading is Fundamental.

Let children see you reading.

Read books together, even after a child has learned how to read.

Take books to use time wisely on long road trips.

Look into Laura Bush's Ready to Read, Ready to Learn.

Attend the annual Texas Book Festival in Austin, founded by Laura Bush.

Attend the National Book Festival in Washington, DC founded by Laura Bush.

Go Write At The Light

One of the many benefits of being an author is being able to choose the subjects of your writing. Since this is my book, and writing is a subject about which I am very passionate, I feel the need to briefly discuss writing as a tool for celebrating a child. Writing is a lifeline for every child. If that sounds like I'm being dramatic, think about how quickly a person, who can't write, gets written off in this world.

Writing goes hand in hand with success, communication, education, and emancipation. It can show a child the way into something positive, or show them the way toward freedom, out of a negative situation. Good writing skills not only offer a child a fast track to self-discovery, but also increase the chances that a child will like what they find in the mirror. Good writing will also help them to find and develop their inner passion and creativity.

As soon as I began in high school to tell others I was interested in a television career, I heard "war stories" of how competitive my chosen industry was. Had I let those negative images deter me, I never would have given myself the chance to fail. Nor would I have given myself the countless opportunities to enjoy the sweet taste of success and experience I've had in my career spanning 20 years and counting! I share this so you'll remember never to tell a child to shy away from their dreams.

When I began to write my first book, *KIDS RULE! The Hopes and Dreams of 21st Century Children*, I quickly discovered that publishing was a far more competitive industry than even television! Nonetheless, I believed I had something to say and knew I could be a good author. Maybe reading this will inspire you to write or to encourage and support a child who likes to write.

Besides learning about rejection and the endless tales of writers having to overcome it, another valuable lesson I learned was that writers are a "community." Sure, we all carry defenses and insecurities, but for the most part, writers support each other. One priceless "perk" of enduring the trials and tribulations as an aspiring (and perspiring) writer is that many established authors, literary agents, and editors often give their time to help writers who are lost or stuck in traffic behind them on the road to publishing success. Perhaps, you could do this too in your line of work. Why not celebrate "children" in your chosen field by becoming an adviser or mentor?

One of the common suggestions given to writers is to write for one hour every day. This is a great way to become dedicated to the craft. It can also help to speed up the lengthy process of writing a book. However, this system never worked for me, because of work. I usually have too much going on doing school and media appearances, giving speeches, serving on advisory boards for charities, and covering my assignments as a television journalist.

I succeed as a highly intuitive writer who is far more satisfied when I write only at times I feel inspired. I named my system, "Go Write at the Light!" When that light of inspiration turns on, I go! And by golly, you'd best get out of my way! I'll scramble for pen and paper no matter where I am or what I'm doing. I'll jot down ideas on a napkin. I'll dash home to my computer. I'll write like there's no tomorrow because during those times, there isn't. There is only today. I am fully alive in those moments. They are rare gifts worth cherishing and celebrating.

For what it's worth, I relied mainly on my intuition in writing this book. Sure, I had notes and quotes from all of the interviews I conducted, but never once did I write an outline or plans for a story. Nor did I even do it for the order in which things appear in the book. I simply felt my way from cover to cover.

Go Write At The Light

Here are some ways you can celebrate a child through writing:

Stress the importance of writing to a child.

Write letters to a child.

Encourage a child to write letters to you.

Write love notes to a child.

Encourage a child to write love notes to you.

Write poems to a child.

Encourage a child to write poems to you.

Make or buy cards for a child.

Encourage a child to make or buy cards for you.

Write an oath to a child.

Have a child write an oath to you.

Write a set of house rules as a family.

Keep a daily journal to help yourself.

Encourage a child keep a daily journal.

Write keepsake books about a child.

Encourage a child to write keepsake books, too.

Write a children's book.

Support "I Love to Write Day" on November 15.

During author visits to schools, children have often suggested to me that it would be really cool if I were to put kid's names in a book. So, I'll plant the seed that one of the ways you can celebrate a child in your life is to become an author, and give them the thrill of having their name published in a book like I'm going to do right now!

Josh Baldrick	Aubrey Goertel
Tara Baldrick	Claire Goertel
Alexa Dectis	Maddie Goertel
Nicole Dectis	Paul Goertel
Buck Dickgraber	Kevin Gower
Jesse DiLeo	Mikki Havlish
Jade DiSciullo	Madison Hrin
Andrew Dubs	Samantha Liney
Meredith Dubs	Alex Lynn
Molly Dubs	Kyra Lynn
Tyler Dubs	Madison Lynn
Briana Druding	Brian Oleksiak
Caitlin Druding	Katie Oleksiak
Corey Druding	Kevin Oleksiak
Eric Druding	Laura Oleksiak
Kimmie Druding	Lauren Oleksiak
Maura Druding	Madeline Oleksiak
Megan Druding	Matthew Oleksiak
Michael Druding	Mary Kate Oleksiak
Nicholas Druding	Sarah Oleksiak
Samantha Druding	Daniel Oleksiuk
Shannon Druding	Mark Oleksiuk
Zachary Druding	Mary Ellen Oleksiuk
Ann Marie Eckerle	Jimmy Queen
Carolyn Eckerle	Amber Raucheisen
Katherine Eckerle	Rachel Raucheisen
Frankie Edwardi	Brandon Shapiro
Collin Fergus	Briann Sicile
Mary Fergus	Truman Schwartzberg
Denton Fergus	Heather Thaler

One Light, One Life

Inside Cameron Logan, a green light was on when it came to writing. No teacher had to force this high schooler to write an essay for class. He loved to pen essays on a variety of philosophical subjects just as a way of expressing himself.

Cameron had set his sights on becoming a writer, or a journalist. Perhaps, he'd be a teacher, too. Another green light Cameron chose to follow altered those career plans, but it was an adjacent red light that made them all go away.

It's a good thing Cameron likely never knew what hit him. Members of the emergency team who cut his 18-year old body from the car, told his mother he never spoke or even moaned. Mercifully, there was no time for suffering in Cameron's sudden final moments. On the other hand, there would be nothing but time for such a burden to be assumed by Cameron's family and friends, and the underage drunk girl behind the wheel who smashed broadside into the driver's side door of his car at a speed of roughly 80 miles per hour.

Cameron's mother, Connie, introduced herself to me while I was signing copies of my book, *KIDS RULE! The Hopes and Dreams of 21st Century Children* at a benefit for The Salvation Army Toy Drive. Every year, the program helps Santa Claus to get presents to even the poorest of kids at Christmas.

As Connie began to tell me about her son who was taken from her less than two years before, I couldn't help but confront the similarities he shared with me. Our common ground went well beyond choosing the same field of work. Like me, Cameron was a relentless observer. He could read people well, and others trusted him and his advice. Children were drawn to him like a "Pied Piper." He also had a sense of humor, including the ability to laugh at himself.

Cameron Logan, flashing the smile his mom says was a fixture.

What I really find uncanny is that I also was in a very serious automobile accident involving a drunk driver during my senior year of high school. Like Cameron, I too died. I left my body as I flew through a tunnel on the other side toward a blinding white light. The only difference between me and Cameron happens to be that I was told I couldn't stay.

For years, Cameron had told his mom, "You never know when you're going to die. You can't put things off." This was his reasoning as to why he should take a break before starting college. He wanted so much to see the world, meet people, and discover cultures that would be new to him. As Connie explained in this frequently debated issue through Cameron's high school years, he would have plenty of time to travel after college.

Eight days before he died, Cameron and Connie had the travel talk for the final time. It was a much different version, explains Connie. "We had just completed the part of the journey where teenage angst divides a parent and child. We had gotten back on a solid footing and were sharing ideas. We certainly didn't agree on everything, but we did agree to respect and love each other," she said.

As they sat at brunch, Connie could clearly see Cameron didn't seem too thrilled about his decision to attend the University of Utah from a number of scholarship offers he received. Cameron's powers of persuasion finally won out. Connie told him, "Sometimes Moms makes mistakes, and if you want to travel, that would be fine. You'll have to pay your own way and work your way around. But, you can put off school until January." Connie said, "He was so excited. That wonderful smile of his was a fixture."

What instantly became a fixture to me was hearing from Connie about a boy who lived a parallel life to mine. I thought even more of how this boy who loved to write and a mother who hoped to some day have her deceased son's work published. I knew I could celebrate him.

Cameron's mother now celebrates her son's life through work as an advocate to eradicate drunk driving. She gives speeches and often reads from his writings. I asked Connie to send me some of his works. Before I told her why I wanted them, I knew I would include one in this book. While I can do nothing to get Connie back her Cameron, I can give her the joy of knowing her son is now a published writer.

If you'll give Cameron's thought provoking essay a chance, you'll see he has not only become a writer, but a teacher, too.

WHY?

By Cameron Logan

Why? Why do we try so hard to do what's right? Why must we follow society to a "t"? Is what's good for the masses always good for the individual?

Is there more to life, and if so, why do we make ourselves miss it? Why? Why must we believe that what we don't understand is wrong? Why?

Why can't we be open and honest and show the world? Why are we shackled by our own insecurities? Why isn't everyone his or her own person? Why isn't everyone part of the group?

Why can't love be clear, can't hate be erased, and truth be all knowing? Why? Why do we cry at a man's funeral if they are going to heaven? Why? Why can't we express our thoughts with ease?

Why can't creativity be key and put knowledge in the background? Does school detract from the creative minds of our youth? Why?

Why can't we see life as a happy beginning? Why can't death be a happy ending? Why?

Why do we assert the need for rules? Why do we sue people, when they are going through the same problems that we are? Why does democracy have so many rules, and so little freedom? Why is there a freedom of speech, but a constriction of thought? Why isn't speech making a point, when you must be politically correct? Why is it "politically" correct?

(continued)

Why is fired "laid off"? Why is crippled "physically disabled"? Why is killed "deceased"? Why? Why?

Why must I write this down when I know everyone else is thinking it? Why are we skeptics, politics, and pragmatics prevailing? Why are we positive, happy, and sunny? Why? Why do we ask why? Why? Why are we here? Why are we alive? Why must we die? I don't know so I ask why.

How come? How do we believe? How do we forget? How come we need to explain how we were created?

How come children have all the fun? How come parents always seem stressed?

How come happiness isn't the focus? How come competition is? How come we give ultimate attention to athletes who better nothing but themselves? How come my mom isn't praised and honored for the love and passion she puts into the teaching of others? How come?

How come we praise the freedoms of our own country, but strip those same freedoms for those outside? How come? I don't know so I ask how come.

Love, hate, tyranny, ecstasy, pain, happiness, suffering, severance, faith, fear, insecurity, love, lust, comfort, coherent, blind, seeing, knowing, trusting, believing, convening, condemning, denying, lying, loving, believing, loving, believing, loving, believing, sweet, disgusted, delighted, ignited, love, pain, believing, dying, living, acknowledge, forgo, completing. Why ask why? How come? Because we can and because we do.

Creating Little Creative Types

Here are some ways you can help to develop the creative juices of a child. Cultivating these skills will be an asset in all aspects of life from career opportunities to personal situations. A good sense of creativity can help to generate a real foundation for confidence, positive thinking and problem solving.

Visit museums with a child.

Suggest a child take music lessons.

Try soothing a child with the sounds of Mozart.

Teach a child to meditate.

Don't force the things you want a child to like.

Paint with a child.

Do pottery with a child.

Play chess with a child.

Develop your own healthy "mind games" with a child.

Take a child to a magic show to show anything is possible.

Teach a child that worrying doesn't help at all.

Give a child applause when deserved.

Dream aloud with a child.

J.L.G. –Jaclyn Lacey Gyger– "Junior Loving Giver"

"I want her to be a kid, too!" In speaking of her only child, Susanna Gyger, appears to say this more out of hope than belief. Like every other nine-year old on the planet, Jaclyn Lacey Gyger can be quite a handful for her mother. Also, like every other nine-year old, she doesn't being told "no." Where this energetic, outgoing nine-year old differs is, the fits she gives her mother stem from her wanting to help everyone! Jaclyn is indeed one child worth celebrating.

Taking after her grandparents who travel the world as missionaries, Jaclyn has launched a mission of her own. She is active in girl scouts, her church choir, bible study, donating her toys and clothes to children in Africa, and so on, and so on, and so on. Believe me when I tell you, Little Miss Gyger against the Salvation Army might just be a fair fight! "Usually, I go around and ask neighbors if they want me to rake leaves or mow the lawn," Jaclyn says. "I tell them they don't have to pay me, but they usually do anyway. Most times, I just put the money back in their mailbox." Does this sound like a typical nine-year old to you?

"Old people, I just feel sad for them," cries Jaclyn. "They're doing all the work and they just can't bend down and stuff. I go to a nursing home the first Sunday of each month. Miss Diane works in the snack bar and I help her. I also help the old people to reach things. I think they feel happy that I do things for them."

Susanna claims, "After Jaclyn does nice things for others, I ask her how she feels. She says, 'I feel really good, mom.' We're turning into a me, me, me society, but not Jaclyn. She wants no part of it. "

This little girl is also a proud American. Each Memorial Day, she places flags on the graves of veterans. On the 2002 holiday, Jaclyn got to ride with the mayor in her town's parade, and was the

Thomas with the patriotic Gyger girls.
Photo by M. Magoo.

MY HANDS ARE TOO SMALL...BUT MY HEART IS BIG.....

My name is Jaclyn and I am 9 years old...
In an effort to help those affected by the recent tragedies,
I am trying to raise money to send

I am asking that if you can donate anything,
Please put it in the attached envelope.
Your donation, BIG or small may save someone's life.

THANK YOU

P.S. PLEASE MAKE SURE TO DISPLAY WITH PRIDE OUR AMERICAN FLAG!

first girl to lead the Pledge of Allegiance in their annual salute to those who gave their lives for our country.

Jaclyn's patriotism comes from having a single mom who has spent 15 years in the United States Air Force. Susanna Gyger works in air crew life support in the Air National Guard. While she was serving in active duty in the Middle East during the war in Afghanistan, young Jaclyn was already busy with her own active duty here at home.

"On 9-11, I was like oh no," said Jaclyn. "I got scared because I thought it was fake, but it wasn't. So, when my mom picked me up from school, I asked her if she would take me to New York to help the firefighters."

Jaclyn thought she had a great idea and wanted to help find survivors trapped in the rubble of the toppled World Trade Center. "The firefighters are probably too big and can't get into real tiny, tight spots. Me and other kids can," she thought. "Kids could even get little firefighters suits, too."

September 11, 2001, was one of those days when Jaclyn really didn't want to hear "no." "She was very upset," recalls her mother. "I explained how searching for survivors in the rubble was too dangerous. She could get killed. Jaclyn's response was that it wasn't fair because grownups always get to do everything. So, I told her she could think of something else to do. That's when she decided raising money was the next best way to help."

Armed with only an envelope and a desire to make a difference, the little patriot was able to hit up neighbors on her block for about $100 in the first few days after 9-11. "And I was like, Wow! I just thought that was great," Jaclyn says.

In less than a month, she raised $753.30. Among her donations were: $ 285.29 for the firefighters, $ 158.00 for the Red Cross, and $ 158.01 for the Salvation Army. Jaclyn proudly says, "I got the one cent from a little boy who was with his mom. He said the penny was all he had, but he wanted to give it to help."

Not all children are as eager to celebrate the good deeds of Jaclyn Lacey Gyger. She admits, "My classmates don't love me. They say, ew, that I do all this stuff. I guess they think it's weird for me to care about what I do for other people."

Another situation affects Jaclyn. She has had no contact from her father since she was nine months old. So, what does she do about it? Jaclyn likens herself to kids who lost their father on 9-11 saying, "Sure, we all wish we had a dad, but hopefully we'll just get to see how special our moms really are."

For the first anniversary of the 9-11 tragedies, Jaclyn went to a pair of local memorials and raised another $ 152.00 in donations. However, in a sign that is good for society, but bad for her mom, Jaclyn is expanding her mission to reach more people and more causes. "She's really been after me," says Susanna. "She's so upset about graffiti in town. She says, 'Mom, do you think we can go clean that up?' Now, she also wants us to pick up cans so we can recycle. But I tell her that we're not picking up trash everywhere we go. I've got to try to set a limit to this stuff, you know." Oh Susanna, best of luck on that one!

Variety Is The Spice Of Life

*"Please help take care of my baby. Her name is Catherine.
I can no longer take care of her. I have eight others.
My husband is out of work. She was born on Thanksgiving Day.
I have always heard of the goodness of show business
and I pray you will look out for her."*

—A Heartbroken Mother

These words were written on a note pinned to the dress of a one-month old baby girl abandoned at the Sheridan Theatre in Pittsburgh on Christmas Eve, 1927. Eleven Godfathers "adopted" the infant and agreed to underwrite her support and education. They named her Catherine Variety Sheridan, in honor of the theatre and their social group known as "The Variety Club."

Much good has come from that gut-wrenching situation. Variety, The Children's Charity, now has more than 15,000 members around the world. It has raised more than one billion dollars through its mission to *help disabled and disadvantaged children lead more comfortable lives, and grow to be productive, self-sufficient adults.*

The Variety Club's first fundraising event on behalf of children was a circus, and the organization still uses circus terms today. Each of the more than fifty chapters is called a "tent," with each president affectionately known as the "Chief Barker."

Originally, one had to work in the entertainment industry to be a member. True to form for its foundation, each Variety Club tent puts on one heck of a show every single day by celebrating and serving children in their local area, who are sick, disabled or disadvantaged.

Variety Club raises funds through events ranging from black tie galas to pig races, gold heart pin sales, golf tournaments, auctions, and telethons. "Unfortunately, telethons are generally a dying breed," says Dr. Ronald Pennock, Chairman of Variety Club in the United States. www.usvariety.org

I can remember watching the great Monty Hall when he used to host the Variety Club Telethon in Philadelphia, but that event went off the air more than a decade ago. The influences of cable and the internet have made television a much more competitive industry. With thousands of channels and websites available, every TV station and network must fight harder for a smaller piece of the pie. Most TV outlets can't afford to give away airtime, and most telethons have become too costly for the charities to pay to keep them going.

In New York City, Variety Club Tent 35 does a mini-telethon on a Sunday afternoon. "Cousin" Bruce Morrow gets enough support from the local entertainment community that the event on WPXN-TV 31 raises a few million dollars for needy kids in New York, New Jersey and Connecticut in only five hours.

Having a background in television, I became so turned on by my experience of celebrating children through the Variety Club Telethon, I simply had to write about these few 20-plus hour loving dinosaurs that refuse to become extinct.

Many wonder, "Why would anyone live in Buffalo?" There are many reasons, but I'll give you a great one for starters. *Buffalo is the home of the longest running locally produced telethon in the world!* Trust me, the western New York city is so much more than the home of chicken wings and winter whiteouts.

People in Buffalo have a deep sense of pride about who they are and where they choose to live. Maybe they are in denial. Maybe they find strength in uniting against what outsiders think. Or maybe, just maybe, those who call Buffalo home, really do love it. (I do, too!) Other communities should be so lucky.

"Buffalo is besieged with negative images from snow to the Super Bowl losses," admits John DiSciullo, programming and promotion director of WKBW-TV. "But the Variety Club Telethon is one undeniably positive thing accomplished by people coming together. Here, it involves all walks of life, the hearts of the regular folks, and the hearts of the rich."

If you shuffle off to Buffalo in the dead of winter, you can bask in the heartfelt warmth of the annual Variety Club Telethon. Producer Steve Podosek says, "The telethon is an icon. It is family. We have a staff of four, and a board of directors of 21, but on Buffalo News Kid's Day we have over 6,000 people get up at 3:00 a.m. They put on layers of clothes, stand outside in the cold and snow for hours, and raise $150,000 selling special edition copies of the Buffalo News to drivers passing by." This is big-hearted Buffalo celebrating its children.

Built on the strength and pride of the community, the Variety Club of Buffalo, Tent 7, was chartered in 1934. For nearly 30 years, it focused on getting equipment for polio victims, handicapped children and premature infants. Fundraising was done primarily through collections, bingo games, and dinner parties. In 1962, change was necessary. "We had run out of ways to raise money," says Jim Hayes, the chapter's president. "We tried collecting at hockey games and movie theatres, but people got really mad at us."

The chapter was battling complications from its enlarged heart. Pressure was mounting from a commitment to raise $50,000 to start a local rehabilitation center. It was a huge amount of money then. "We knew if disabled kids had problems or got sick, they were sent into a corner and put by themselves. Variety Club and Dr. Robert Warner believed every child is as good as every other," says Jim Hayes. "We took responsibility for these families and gave them better ways to cope and live."

Out of town public relations executives told the tent's board of directors it might make a wad of money if they stayed on TV all night. Jim Hayes admits, "We weren't too sure." As fate would have it, sitting on the board was Van DeVries, general manager of WGR-TV, the NBC affiliate in Buffalo. He decided the idea was worth a try.

Lorne Greene, star of "Bonanza," America's top-rated TV show at the time, hosted the first Variety Club Telethon. Jim Hayes said they grossed a whopping sum of about $107,000. But, getting the financial windfall went about as smoothly as a barrel ride over the nearby Niagara Falls.

"Thousands wanted to come to the studio, but it wasn't big enough to handle it," says Jim Hayes. "So many people were calling in pledges that telephone lines were knocked out of commission, including those of police and hospitals. There were front-page headlines that our telethon stopped emergencies. It was a disaster for us. Van told us we would never get a chance to do that to him or his TV station again."

WKBW-TV, an ABC affiliate, was newly on the air. Channel 7 eagerly became the home of the telethon in 1963 and will likely never let it go. "It's such a legacy. There's so much we do on the air that is on and gone," says Bill Ransom, general manager. "This has long lasting impact. It is real-life television with real emotion involved."

Real people, real local, this is the telethon's formula for success in Buffalo. Today, success means it raises roughly $1.5 million per year to support a variety of causes from the Warner Rehabilitation Center and other programs at the Children's Hospital of Buffalo, to cancer research, to schools and camps for handicapped and underprivileged kids.

"It's not what you'd think the public would storm behind, but the key is to have the telethon as a thank you parade," says Executive Director, Richard Goldstein, who has served the Variety Club of Buffalo for more than 25 years. "You wouldn't get the money year-round without the telethon, so we take the time to thank each and every donor and organization. The guy who runs a spaghetti dinner is treated the same as the union guy who brings in a check for $50,000." (I swear it's true.)

When I first appeared as one of the hosts on the Variety Club Telethon and donated the proceeds from sales of my book, there was quite a unique celebrity cast. The kid lovers included the Channel 7 personalities, Buffalo Bills great Jim Kelly, singer Oleta Adams, and soap opera star Wally Kurth, of ABC's "General Hospital." Richard Goldstein admits it is always a unique mix. "The viewers see Bowzer from Sha Na Na come back and think he likes Buffalo. They see Mr. Food each year and think he likes Buffalo. You could never, never, never, ever have those two starring in a telethon somewhere else. If you tried, they'd look at you like you were from Mars!"

Celebrity Child "Sporty" Watson talking with Buffalo boxer, Baby Joe Mesi.

Celebrity Child Erin Deering talking with Thomas Baldrick.

Victoria Macy with "Mr. Food." The girl with a brain tumor walked five miles through her neighborhood to collect over $3,000 so she and others can enjoy Variety Club summer camps.

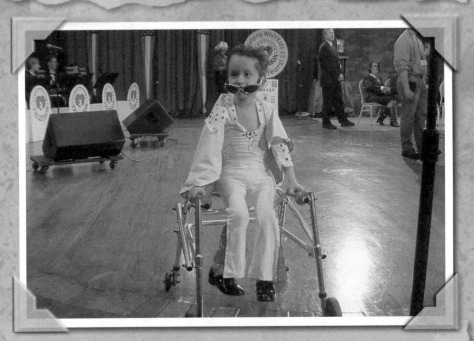

Celebrity Child Tyler Ball having a ball as "Little Elvis."

There are many hard-working members like Sam Gikas and Raymond Carr who are Variety Club of Buffalo heroes. There are also others in the community such as Tony Billoni, star of Channel 7's late-night movie show, "Offbeat Cinema." He runs the annual "Variety Rocks" charity concert that is great for raising money and a sense of caring with the next generation. But without a doubt, it is the little stars that shine the brightest on the telethon.

10-year old Erin Deering was born with spina bifida. She is one of the telethon's celebrity children. "The telethon helps me to think I'm a regular kid, and not just a disabled kid," says Erin. "It makes me happy to think that everybody is working just to make the kids happy. I come back every year to help the kids who don't have it as lucky as I do."

"Erin has so much confidence now, and much of it has to do with Variety Club. She has such a true heart and is so proud to be a part of the telethon," claims her mother, Jennifer Deering. "Erin was such a blessing. We were told she wasn't going to live. Now, Erin feels like she can accomplish anything."

I celebrate the Deerings for working as counselors with families of newborns like Erin. Jennifer says, "It's discomforting to have a child born with spina bifida, but not depressing. We want other parents to know that a normal life is still possible. It will just have a few kinks in it. But what family doesn't?"

"Seeing what children are capable of is why so many work so hard all year. Once, during the telethon," recalls Chief Barker Diane Kuciel, the first woman to serve as telethon chairperson, "Erin and a boy named Sporty Watson who were supposedly never going to walk," had worked really hard to surprise our chairpersons. Erin walked over to Patty Somogey, and Sporty walked to Sam Gikas." Steve Podosek adds, "You could have heard a pin drop. There were no words to describe the feeling in that room and in rooms across Western New York, Southern Ontario, and Northwestern Pennsylvania where TV's were tuned in."

John DiSciullo of WKBW-TV remembers that public milestone and has his own more private one about "Daddy's little girl." The Executive Producer of the telethon has been glued to the event for more than twenty years, but just a couple of years ago, his only child was born two months premature. "Jade was having real trouble breathing and she had to be given surfactant therapy (lubrication) which helped to make it easier. My family needed that therapy which was developed right here in Buffalo. We needed the equipment that Variety Club dollars helped to pay for. It was a great comfort knowing the telethon played a role in keeping my baby alive."

Why remember Buffalo for the infamous "wide right" that would have won Super Bowl XXV? Why not remember Buffalo for using wide-open arms to embrace needy children? Why tease Buffalo about which weekend is boating season on Lake Ontario? Why not back Buffalo on the weekend of their 21-hour long Variety Club Telethon? www.variety.buffnet.net

"If somebody here realizes they'll be helping a child, I can't remember ever hearing the word 'no' in more than twenty years with Variety Club," says Diane Kuciel. "Buffalo is such a caring city. We've lost jobs, but people always help. If they can't help financially, they ask what else they can do."

"It's the public's telethon. They own it and are very protective of it," says Executive Director, Richard Goldstein. "Stores close, the economy here is bad, star athletes come and go. But this telethon is a forever. It's like people say, 'You don't touch my telethon.' It gives the people of Buffalo much needed pride in themselves."

At the Variety Club of Iowa, "We start every year flat broke," celebrates Past President, Stan Reynolds. "There is no saving for a rainy day. We spend every dollar we make every year on helping kids." Since 1937, they have created more than 50 million ways to prove it.

The annual telethon has been the cornerstone of fundraising for Tent 15 since 1975. It supports more than 200 special programs and charities throughout Iowa and neighboring states. The beneficiaries are children's hospitals, youth at risk, and thousands of disabled and disadvantaged infants and kids.

Thank goodness the hearts are bigger than the TV egos in the heartland of America. Though the telethon hub is WOI-TV, Channel 5 in Des Moines, the 22-hour program is simulcast on KCRG-TV in Eastern Iowa, KCAU-TV in Sioux City, and WHBF-TV in

The Variety Club of Iowa Telethon shows the true Heartland of America.

Quad Cities. Over 200 cable systems carry the telethon, so it reaches about 85% of the state. More importantly, it raises roughly $4 million annually for kids.

"We have a cast bigger than Gone With the Wind," laughs Stan Reynolds. As a specialist in insurance for the movie industry, Stan ought to know. He has written and produced the Iowa telethon for nearly thirty years. "Our cast features people you've never heard of, as well as stars like Emma Samms, and former NFL greats Ben Davidson and Ed Podolak. Once they come, they come back."

An additional team of 22 well-known types, like football coaches, politicians, and business leaders annually generate more than one million dollars themselves in this celebration of a child. These VIP'S (very interested people) work the front row of the telephone bank. Each VIP has a personal phone number that viewers can call to talk directly with them, and, of course to make a pledge.

"Telethons are dinosaurs," admits Ray Johnson, who has served as director of the WOI-TV event for nearly thirty years. "I just think most people in Iowa are givers not takers. There's a family lifestyle and attitude here. It's a friendly state, and when you get as many VIP's to appear on a telethon as we do, it's something that just sustains itself year after year."

The Iowa Grocery Industry Association has a great coupon redemption program, "Cash for Kids." Cars and gasoline are donated to help the telethon, as is food for the roughly 3,000 people who work on the telethon. "It's a well-oiled machine that has gotten easier over the years," says Stan Reynolds.

They must like to do everything big out in the open of the "Hawkeye State." Who can forget the one family Variety Club helped? On November 19, 1997, Bobbi and Kenny McCaughey became the proud parents of Kenneth, Alexis, Natalie, Kelsey, Brandon, Nathan, and Joel. They were the world's first surviving septuplets!

Stan Reynolds is happy to say that the McCaughey seven spent their early days under watchful eyes in the Variety Club Nursery in the neo natal intensive care unit of the children's hospital. I told you the man specialized in insurance!

In nearby St. Louis, Variety Club Tent 4 www.varietystl.com mainly feeds its funding needs with an annual telethon and a "Dinner With the Stars," featuring big names like the legendary Ray Charles, the lovely Bernadette Peters, Kenny Rogers, and The Temptations. For more than a dozen years, the kind folks at KMOV-TV, Channel 4 haven't been able to resist the temptation of donating full support in producing the telethon.

Since it was founded in1932, the St. Louis Variety Club has raised well over $50 million from the caring community. Each year, Tent 4 helps more than 200,000 disabled and disadvantaged children in the Greater St. Louis area. It provides funding for behavioral counseling, hospitals, schools, camps, day care, clubs and community centers, and essential equipment such as wheelchairs, prostheses, and leg braces. Like Variety Club tents everywhere, it also has many special sunshine coaches on the streets of St. Louis, transporting children to important medical appointments and enriching community events.

Now, we must go north of the border. The show of shows when it comes to Variety Club Telethons may very well be the Show of Hearts Telethon in British Columbia. Since going on the air in 1965, it has raised more than $100 million for disabled and disadvantaged kids. www.variety.bc.ca

Broadcast live province-wide in a working partnership with the giving people at Global Television, the 23-hour fundraiser now averages nearly $ 2 per head from the population of 3.5 million in British Columbia. "Our telethon is a source of real money, not a thank you parade," points out George Pitman, the Vice-President of Variety Club International, who has worked on the telethon for thirty years. "We have done $ 2 million in phone calls during the 23-hour period. We use net numbers not gross, and if you phone in a $500 pledge, we call you back to verify it. Credibility is a big reason for our success."

Credibility proved big in 2002 when the Variety Club of British Columbia received notification that it was the benefactor of a $1.5 million estate from a 55-year old woman who died of breast cancer. She left half her money to a cancer clinic and the other half to Variety Club. Amazingly, there were no records to indicate that the woman had ever made a donation to Variety Club when she was alive. She said her decision was based on giving to a credible, trustworthy organization that helped kids all across the province.

Here are a couple of examples of how her money will celebrate a child: Five-year old Derek is one of the Canadian kids that Variety Club works for daily. He was born with cerebral palsy. He loves the Vancouver Canucks and hopes to one day play hockey. Medicare does not pay for the braces Derek needs to stand straight on his feet and to walk. It is Variety Club that stands tall for Derek. It is Variety Club that is getting him closer to his hockey goal.

Some may view Courtney's condition as a different form of the "Terrible Two's," but not her. The precious two-year old always wears a smile even though she was born with hip dysplasia (a congenital abnormal development). Her hips were surgically repaired as an infant, but she still cannot walk. Courtney needs special therapy. The Variety Club of British Columbia provides the private water-physiotherapy that is stretching Courtney's leg muscles so one day she can walk with her big sisters.

In 2000, this telethon changed its format and stopped using live entertainment. Now, it gets permission to air taped concerts and performances like The Three Tenors, The Three Divas, and the best of Shania Twain. The plan has worked.

No matter how they do it, no matter where, Variety Club is music to the ears of families with a child in need. (They do help deaf kids to hear, too!) If you ever have the opportunity to see the magic of kids enjoying themselves at a Variety Club summer camp like I have at the one in Philadelphia, it is something you surely will never forget. Everybody fits in at these special camps. They all have fun as kids, not as kids with disabilities.

The Variety Club creed is *"No one stands taller than when helping a child."* I work with Variety Club. Perhaps, if you do the same, you'll agree that *Variety is the Spice of Life.*

"Amazing" Grace is all smiles after the Variety Club of British Columbia Telethon.

Cash n' Carry

Give a child a piggy bank.

Give a child a piggyback ride.

Teach a child about money management.

Allow a child to earn an allowance.

Learn about 529 college-saving plans.

Teach a child that money cannot buy happiness.

Teach a child about the dangers of credit card debt.

Let a child receive under pillow payments from "The Tooth Fairy."

Teach a child about the unlimited abundance of the universe.

Enjoy carrying a child every chance you can.

Make sure school bags aren't too heavy for a child to carry.

Sing to all infants and small children.
   (They don't know or care if you can carry a tune!)

Teach a child not to carry a grudge.

Give a child coins to throw into a fountain.

Establish a savings account for a child.

Let a child empty the change into a coin counting machine.

Play a game of monopoly with a child.

Buy U.S. Savings Bonds for a child.

Carry photos of a child wherever you go.

Teach a child not to carry the weight of the world on their
   shoulders.

Use compassion and communication to carry a child through
   hard times.

Food For Thought

Kids love treats. Treats are especially tasty because when you give them, a child feels loved. So please, feed their souls as well as their little bodies with treats. If you do, you'll be celebrating often as you watch children who are happy and healthy on both the inside and out!

Compliment a child for their appearance.

Have fun cooking with a child.

Cook their favorite foods.

Bake cookies with a child.

Take a child to their favorite restaurant.

Treat a child to cotton candy.

Treat a child to a real Coney Island hotdog.

Treat a child to "kiddie champagne" (sparkling cider).

Make an Easter basket for a child.

Create an Easter egg hunt for a child.

Eat meals as a family.

Give thanks or say "Grace" at all meals.

Buy a child a Happy Meal.

Make Jell-o with a child.

Share popcorn with a child.

Have a child taste a classic Philly Cheese Steak.

Enjoy special Thanksgiving dinners.

Take a child trick or treating.

Treat a child to a water ice.

Love And Happiness Are Like Sticky Peanut Butter

"Love and happiness remind me of sticky peanut butter. When you spread them around, you can't help but get some on yourself!"

—MARSHA JORDAN

Bearing the initials "MJ" and the last name of Jordan, a 47-year old disabled grandmother from Northern Wisconsin is doing for the internet, what Michael Jordan has done for the game of basketball, lifting it to a higher level. Marsha Jordan is a champion for establishing *The Hugs and Hope Club* www.hugsandhope.com.

Jordan, married for 27 years with one grown son and a spoiled toy poodle, created the online mission to comfort and support children with life threatening illnesses, as well as their families. It is her way of sharing the love of God and making the information highway…super.

"One mom told me she felt like running out into the street yelling, *My Child is sick. Won't somebody please help us?"* says Marsha. Can you imagine that mother's state of despair? Marsha Jordan could, having been through it first-hand with her badly burned little grandson.

It is a blessing that Michael is not the only Jordan hard to stop from succeeding. Marsha battles headaches, muscle and joint pain, and chronic fatigue symptoms of the disease, Lupus. In 1998, she lost her eyesight for several months, but fortunately regained some vision. However, she was no longer able to work or lead an active lifestyle, so weight gain became just another of her daily battles.

Believing God had plans for her time, Marsha took to creating web pages and joining online prayer groups. By the fall of 2000, these two hobbies became linked when she created a web page for a friend who contracted Lou Gehrig's Disease. Thus, the idea for *The Hugs and Hope Club* was born.

126

"It saddens me that parents are so desperately searching for someone to care and to help them through the ordeal of watching their helpless child suffer," says Marsha. "So, I decided to be that someone, and found it's amazing how much I can do."

Each month, her site posts stories and pictures of children who are critically ill. Families often submit information, craving the prayers that can generate miracles. The hundreds of visitors each day to the site are asked to say a prayer for the children, to mail a card or small gift, or to pass along a note of encouragement to the parents. "Anyone can help," claims Jordan. "Whatever your talent, you can use it to benefit suffering children or their families."

The Hugs and Hope Club sends happy mail to the families of children like Fahad, a three-year old stricken with a rare blood disorder. Then, there's Nathan and his little brother P.J., who battle the fatal Batten's Disease. Annabelle, a two-year old recovering from the surgical removal of her cancerous left eye is proof of the power of this simple work. Tearing open her box of "happy mail," she yells "Mama, look! It's a teddy bear!" The bear, along with stickers, books, and other goodies, accomplished something that hadn't happened in quite a while, it caused little Annabelle to smile.

Jordan now has the support of a true, but unheralded all-star team made up of more than five-hundred volunteers from coast to coast. In the East, there's Jan, a graphic artist and cancer survivor. She uses her talent to make web art for kids. In the South, Sue Gene packs a whole lot of love into the boxes of toys she mails. Tiffany gives from deep in the heart of Texas, as she moderates a chat room for parents to vent frustrations and find camaraderie.

The Hugs and Hope Club does not have the high visibility or clout of other children's charities. Nor, does it have regional chapters or branches. It relies solely on ordinary people doing extraordinary things for those who need it most.

I wanted to share this story with you because it is a celebration of terminally ill children, and where they are at in the moment. It does not offer a cure. What it does is prove that anyone can make a difference in the life of a child. It offers hugs, something we can always use. It also offers prayers and hope, things we always need.

The Druding kids enjoying their ride in "the limbo."

Be A Crazy Uncle Tommy

Be a crazy Aunt Marie, or a crazy mom, dad, grandma or grandpa. Whoever you are to a child, do something silly with them. You'll both enjoy these times and remember them long after you've forgotten many other moments in life.

Do a "limbo!" Every year after Christmas, my little cousins (Megan, Caitlin, Corey, Kimmie, Shannon, Maura and Briana) get to go to the ice show when it comes to town. The year we went to Toy Story on Ice was different though. As we were getting ready to leave from my Uncle Harry's house, the kids noticed something through the window. What pulled up right out front was a white stretch limousine!

I'll never forget the reactions of the little eyes filled with wonder as I nonchalantly walked outside and said, "Okay, who's coming with me?" The kids didn't know what to do. They thought I was just being crazy again. When they realized that the limo was there for them, they were jumping and giggling and couldn't contain their excitement.

It was first-class accommodations all the way as I had brought along plenty of snacks, treats, candy and bottles of their favorite "Kid Champagne." (sparkling cider) We had so much fun that the kids couldn't wait for the ice show to end so we could get back into the limo for the drive home. The four-year old twins, Maura and Briana, were saying, "I want to go back in the limbo!"

None of us will ever forget that day, including the limo driver who said he'd seen a lot of things on the job, but never something like this! One of my relatives asked me why I was doing something that was such a waste of money. My reply was "To put big smiles on little faces."

Be A Crazy Uncle Tommy

Play a real sloppy game of football in the mud.

Make imprints of a child's precious little hands, feet or "Tiny Hiney" in cement.

Reward a child with spontaneous days of special fun and adventure with you.

Run yourselves silly in a game of "Duck, Duck, Goose."

Play hard at "Hide & Seek."

Play a game of Twister.

Blast favorite songs on the car radio and sing your hearts out.

Do impressions of animals at the zoo.

Tickle each other.

Do whatever it takes to make you both giggle.

Jump for joy on a trampoline.

Create shows that you videotape.

Create a really cool bedroom for a child.

Let a child bury you in the sand.

Build a colossal sand castle. Don't worry about it being washed away. The time you spend together building it is what matters and lasts forever.

Make any day Halloween! Some days, I choose to brighten the world by wearing my Super hero costume. When people stop laughing enough to ask me, "Why are you wearing that?" I casually reply, "Why not?"

Yes Sir!

When Sir Winston Churchill was Prime Minister of Great Britain, he made a few personal visits to the home of President Franklin Delano Roosevelt in Hyde Park, New York. Churchill's visits to the beautiful Hudson Valley were unlike those of other visiting dignitaries because he would give our president fits!

Supposedly, Sir Winston was quite a night owl who liked to have a few drinks. Meanwhile, FDR preferred to work on his stamp collection for a while, before going to bed at an early hour. One night, Churchill was said to have left FDR's house because it was too hot. He chose to cool off and hold court floating in a boat (and dragging the Secret Service along with him) on the Hudson River behind the house.

Perhaps, it was during his late night sessions when Sir Winston Churchill came up with some of his famous sayings. Proudly, I credit him for one of the greatest pieces of wisdom I know, *"We make a living by what we get, but we make a life by what we give."*

Churchill's keen insight is a powerful tool to put into the hands and heart of a child. I know it helps me to clarify my life's mission. I say, "Yes Sir" to Winston's wisdom, and refer to it often to keep me on track. It doesn't mean that I don't want or need money. I do. However, for me, I must believe in the abundance of the universe. I need to know that there is enough of everything to go around for everyone including me.

Countless experiences have diminished my doubts and proven to me that the more you give in life . . . the more you do get yourself. If you can learn to give without attachment to the outcome, you will truly be amazed at all that comes back to you!

I am excited about earning a good living and being rich. I'm just driven more by the longer-lasting rewards of making a life for myself through giving. Perhaps you can try to keep my words or Sir Winston's in mind as you look at these fine charities and causes that celebrate a child each and every day.

Action Alliance for Children www.4children.org
A resource of reliable information for policymakers, children's service providers and advocates, and the media.

Advocates for Youth www.advocatesforyouth.org
Helping young people make informed and responsible decisions about their reproductive and sexual health.

Adopt America Network www.adoptamericanetwork.org
Special children deserve special families.

American Humane Association www.americanhumane.org
Protecting children and animals from abuse and neglect.

Angelcare (formerly Children's Aid International) www.angelcare.org
A band of angels providing poor children with food, medicine, clothing, schooling and disaster relief.

Ann Martin Children's Center www.annmartin.org
Providing psychological and educational services for children and families.

Todd M. Beamer Foundation www.beamerfoundation.org
To equip children experiencing family trauma to make heroic choices every day.

Believe in Tomorrow National Children's Foundation www.grant-a-wish.org
Inspiring critically ill children to believe!

Big Brothers and Big Sisters www.bbbsa.org
Provides positive mentoring relationships for children.

Boys & Girls Clubs of America www.bgca.org
The positive place for kids, especially those disadvantaged.

Boy Scouts of America www.bsa.scouting.org

Cal Farley's Boys Ranch & Affiliates www.calfarley.org
Providing a Christian environment for at-risk boys and girls in Texas and 15 other states.

Campfire Boys & Girls www.campfireboysandgirls.org
Developing motivated and self-confident boys and girls.

Cascade Boys Ranch www.cbr.org
Model of teaching successful living for at-risk boys.

Child Find of America www.childfindofamerica.org
Locating missing children and preventing abduction.

Childhelp USA www.childhelpusa.org
Treatment and prevention of child abuse.

Child Welfare League of America www.cwla.org
Serving abused and neglected Ammerican children and their families.

Children International www.children.org
Overcoming poverty around the world.

Children's Defense Fund www.childrensdefensefund.org
Provides a voice for all children, leaving no child behind.

Children's Heartlink www.childrensheartlink.org
Treatment and prevention of heart disease in needy children.

Children's House at Johns Hopkins www.childrenshouse.org
Home for families with sick children in the Baltimore area.

Children's Mercy Fund www.cmfund.org
Providing emergency food, clothing, medical supplies, equipment, and care to suffering children throughout the world.

Children's Miracle Network www.cmn.org
The alliance of premier hospitals for children.

Children's Relief Network www.romanianchildren.org
Bringing hope to the hurting children of Romania.

Covenant House www.covenanthouse.org
Providing shelter and services to runaway youth.

D.A.R.E. www.dare.com
Drug Abuse Resistance Education cooperative between education and law enforcement.

Dan Bylsma Charitable Trust Fund www.DanBylsma.com
Established by the NHL player.

Families International www.familiesinternational.com
Rhode Island corporation specializing in adopting children from Russia.

Feed the Children www.feedthechildren.org
Feeding the hungry in the U.S. around the world.

Futures for Children www.futurechild.org
Improving the well-being of American Indian children.

Girls and Boys Town www.girlsandboystown.org
Changing the way America cares for her children and families.

Families of SMA www.fsma.org
Finding a cure for Spinal Muscular Atrophy.

Girls Incorporated www.girlsinc.org
Making American girls strong, smart, and bold.

Girl Scouts of the USA www.girlscouts.org
Where girls go strong.

Give Kids the World www.gktw.org
Florida resort for families of children with life-threatening illnesses.

National 4-H Council www.fourhcouncil.edu
Building a world in which youth and adults learn, grow, and work together as catalysts for positive change.

Healing the Children www.healingchildren.org
Envisioning a world where every child has access to medical care.

Heifer International www.heifer.org
Ending hunger and world poverty.

Hugh O'Brian Youth Leadership www.hoby.org
Focusing on high school sophomores.

I Have a Dream Foundation www.ihad.org
Helping children from low-income areas reach their education and career goals.

Junior Achievement www.ja.org
Let their success be your inspiration.

Juvenile Diabetes Research Foundation www.jdrf.org
Dedicated to finding a cure.

Kisses For Kyle Foundation www.kissesforkyle.org
Keeping a child's memory alive by helping sick children.

Make-A-Wish Foundation www.wish.org
Granting the wishes of children with life-threatening illnesses to enrich the human experience with hope, strength, and joy.

March of Dimes www.modimes.org
Saving babies, together.

Marywood Children and Family Services www.marywood.org
Providing shelter and support services to children.

Miracle Flights for Kids www.miracleflights.com
Transporting kids to necessary medical treatment.

National Center for Missing & Exploited Children
www.missingkids.org
Founded by John Walsh in 1984 following the death of his son, Adam.

National Council for Adoption www.ncfa-usa.org
Helping as many children as possible to find permanent homes.

Muscular Dystrophy Association www.mdausa.org
Where hope begins.

Omaha Home for Boys www.omahahomeforboys.org
Strengthening youth and families.

Our Little Brothers and Sisters www.nphamigos.org
Caring for orphaned and abandoned children in Latin America and the Caribbean.

Pearl S. Buck International www.pearl-s-buck.org
Bringing hope to children worldwide.

PLAN International USA (Childreach) www.childreach.org
Helping children shape their world.

Prevent Child Abuse America www.preventchildabuse.org

Project Cuddle www.projectcuddle.org
Preventing the abandonment and death of newborn babies.

Reading is Fundamental www.rif.org
Raising awareness in our homes, classrooms, and communities.

Ronald McDonald House Charities www.rmhc.com
Bettering the lives of children and families around the world.

St. Jude's Children's Research Hospital www.stjude.org
Finds cures for children with catastrophic illnesses through research and treatment.

Save the Children www.savethechildren.org
Working to create opportunities for the world's children to live safe, healthy, and fulfilling lives.

Salvation Army www.salvationarmyusa.org
Preaching the gospel of Jesus Christ, and to meet human needs in His name without discrimination

Shop with a Cop www.tacomapolice.org
Tacoma police officers share Christmas with needy children and families.

Youth Power www.youthpower.org
Helps girls 9-13 to make the most of themselves.

Toys for Tots www.toysfortots.org
U.S. Marine Corps Reserve program delivering hope and new toys to needy children at Christmas.

United Fathers of America www.ufa.org
Helping fathers remain actively involved after divorce or separation.

United Mitochondrial Disease Foundation www.umdf.org
Redefining hope for families affected by mitochondrial diseases.

United Negro College Fund www.uncf.org
A mind is a terrible thing to waste.

Unicef www.unicefusa.org
Promoting the survival, protection, and development of all children worldwide through fundraising, advocacy, and education.

WorldVision www.worldvision.org
Serving the world's poorest children and families in nearly 100 countries.

Tech Check

One could look at the internet like a child. It grows every day before our very eyes. We learn new things about it constantly. We want it to be good and have a positive effect on society and we want it to conform.

Much like a child who quickly outgrows clothes and shoes, the internet and other technologies are growing at a faster rate than our society's knowledge of how to use them. We don't have laws or rules in place to govern and protect us each time there is a technological advancement. But, when it comes to technology and a child, please don't think you have to wait for the folks on Capitol Hill to determine what is right. Those decisions are only made after they figure out who is on the right wing and who is on left!

Do your own tech checks for children. Keep a close eye on their access to technology and establish healthy rules for how they use them. Make technology a friend to you and a child.

Place content blocks on internet access.

Keep computers in an open room in the house.

Send loving emails to a child.

Place content blocks with cable TV.

Shoot you own home videos.

Watch home videos as a family.

Set limits on technology use.

Have "No Tech Nights" in your home or community. Try having family talks, review children's homework, or take walks. Savor and save! Whatever you do on "No Tech Nights," savor those moments in which you simply enjoy being with the people you love. An added benefit is that you'll be saving money on your electric bill!

Know the content of video games.

Play video games with a child.

TV Or Not TV? That Is The Question

I'm not going to give you one good reason why the television should not be a "babysitter" for children. I will give you 100, 000 reasons. The Center for Media Education reports that by the time children complete 6th grade, they will witness more than 100,000 acts of violence on TV, including 8,000 murders. These numbers double by the time they graduate from high school. Is it any wonder that kids who watch too much TV may be prone to violence? Perhaps you can use this section of the book as a new kind of TV Guide.

Don't have a TV set in a child's bedroom.

Don't depend on the TV as a babysitter.

Set healthy limits on the amount of TV time in your home.

Explain to a child that everything on television isn't true or correct.

Make watching TV a shared family activity.

Dads, share the remote!

Watch out for upsetting breaking news live coverage and keep kids away from it. (NOTE: While little ones won't understand TV content, they will become upset if they are sensitive to how others are reacting.)

Seek out helpful programs you want a child to watch.

Show a child how to get to Sesame Street.

Tune in to these sources for more information:

National PTA www.pta.org

Talking with Kids About Tough Issues www.talkingwithkids.org

Children Now www.childrennow.org

Center for Media Education www.cme.org

A Child Is Like A Cell Phone

One morning, while working on this book during a train ride from New Jersey into New York Penn Station, I was in search of the perfect word to strengthen a sentence I had just written about celebrating a child. The more I looked at the screen of my laptop computer, the more frustrated I seemed to become.

I shifted my search to look out the window, but that wasn't working much better. There I was, minding my own business in a silent struggle on behalf of children when all of a sudden, it seemed like the cell phones of fifty passengers started ringing at once. Thoughts of cell phones further interrupted my thinking about kids. Then, I quietly laughed as the idea hit me, a child is like a cell phone!

Once you've gotten used to one, you can't live without it.

You can take both of them anywhere.

You can play games with both of them.

You don't like the feeling of being disconnected.

You shouldn't use them just to hear yourself talk.

You must listen in order to have a conversation.

It's tough to understand what is being said when someone is screaming.

Be sure to recharge them.

It can be costly if you abuse them.

It's a part of life; sometimes you get bad reception. Be patient and seek a better place for clear and open communication with a child like you do with a cell phone.

Remember, you'll feel much better if you use up all of your "anytime minutes" with a child.

Stone Cold Kirk Spencer

His voice commands respect. Immediately. When Kirk Spencer first called me on the telephone, his gruff Texas tone made me feel like an outgunned cowboy shaking in my boots. By the way, all he said was, *"Hello, is this Thomas Baldrick?"*

Kirk Spencer looks as tough as he sounds. At six-feet-four inches tall and weighing 255 pounds, he laughs and admits, "I look like a wrestler." Most people agree. With a goat'ee and shaved head, Kirk is a dead ringer for the former World Wrestling champion, "Stone Cold" Steve Austin. The comparisons end there.

Big, bad, Kirk Spencer is not a wrestler. He is a nurse. Not only that, his specialty is working with children. As I see it, there is only one way the Stone Cold image fits. Kirk Spencer is a "Stone Cold Softee" when it comes to caring for sick little kids. And for that, I proudly celebrate him.

I came to know Kirk in the summer of 2002 when he was featured in the ABC Television series, *"Houston Medical."* My friend, Joel Schwartzberg, was the lead cameraman on the reality-based series. Six one-hour episodes were ordered by the network as a summer series. Viewers were given an all-access look at the every-day dramas of Memorial Hermann Hospital in Houston, Texas, where Kirk Spencer worked.

In watching the first episode, I laughed as Kirk "negotiated" ever so patiently with a precious little patient. The cameras captured a truly tender moment as a four-year old walked off with Nurse Spencer's stethoscope. Although the boy decided it should be *his* new toy, Kirk was able get the stethoscope back without incident. I also cried during the show when they touched on Kirk's story. I knew then and there, it had to be included in this book.

Kirk Spencer, a "Stone Cold Softee" with sick kids.

Kirk Spencer was born in San Jose, California, but has called Houston his home for more than forty years. He played baseball in his younger years, and has been a 1st degree brown belt in judo since age 15. His chosen profession was to be a utility construction worker, performing rigorous tasks such as laying water and sewer lines in the ground. He also built greenhouses. This was how he earned a living for 15 years.

In 1992, Kirk was having difficulty finding steady work. He did whatever odd jobs he could get in order to generate income. For Kirk, it was a time filled with doubts and fears. It was also a golden opportunity to create change. "I was thinking back to 1990 when my stepson, Greg died. I asked myself, *What do I really want to do?*"

The death of a child is a brutal blow to any parent. For the Spencer family, it was especially hard because Greg took his own life after only 13 years. "All we know is that he was depressed. He was a grade behind other kids his age. Greg felt stupid, but we constantly told him he wasn't. Sixth grade can be tough. He was trying to date and was just unsure of himself."

On what seemed like a typical Saturday afternoon, Kirk and the two kids were playing cards. Greg calmly said he didn't want to play anymore. While Kirk and seven-year old Cassie played one more game, Greg went to his room and hung himself from the side of his bunk bed. When his little sister found him, Greg was still alive, but barely.

Kirk performed CPR and was able to restore a heartbeat as they waited for an ambulance. He saved Greg's life, but only temporarily. Despite many believing the hospitalized boy would be all right, Greg passed away 36-hours later. It was the worst kind of Monday morning imaginable.

"What happened with Greg changed my view of caring for people. When I was looking at what I wanted to do with my life, I was remembering how much the family, and one very special nurse showed they cared for Greg. So, I decided, I want to do that, too."

Though Kirk never remembered that nurse's name, he vividly remembers who she was as a person. He fondly recalls her love, patience, and dedication, as she helped Greg, *and* each and every one of the more than 50 family members who formed a vigil at his side.

When Kirk announced his decision to change careers, it got a positive reaction from everyone he told. He went to work as an aide in a nursing home to see if he liked it. He learned right away that he did. Kirk also enrolled at San Jacinto College to study nursing, earning LVN status in 1996. Two years later, he finished up at Alvin Community College and officially became a registered nurse.

In 1999, Kirk Spencer began work as an RN at Memorial Hermann Hospital. "My goal is to make it a good adventure for kids while they are there, so that they aren't afraid of hospitals. They shouldn't be, because hospitals are where we can make them better."

Kids do have many things they can be afraid of in a hospital, but a very tough-looking, tough-sounding male nurse named Mr. Spencer, isn't usually one of them. "I try to be very calming with the children and use my voice as friendly rather than stern. I get on their level and talk to them. I squat down so they know I am talking to them and never tower over them," says Kirk. He laughs in admitting, "When I walk into a room for the first time, I do scare some kids."

Kirk says he can work faster with a child than an adult patient, and also believes the rewards are greater. "Kids are fun to work with because they're more genuine. If they're hurtin', they'll tell you. If they're not, they'll tell you. Kids are very honest when it comes to illnesses. Besides, I get to have fun with them, and joke with them, and play games to help them to feel better."

Kirk claims he has seen one or two nurses bigger than him. However, he is a figure larger than life to many of his little patients and their families. Even the ones scared at first by him, quickly realize how lucky they are to have Kirk Spencer on their side.

"I often ask doctors, '*Are you sure you need that blood, doc?*' Kids don't like needles and the last thing I want to do is hurt them. They feel safe with me because I am as genuine with them as they are with me. Families have confidence in me that I know what I'm doing and that I do my best each and every time. They often prefer to deal with me. Many kids have said they won't let anybody touch them except for me."

A favorite story of Kirk's involves a five-year old girl who was bitten by a dog in Mexico about two weeks before Christmas. No one was able to test the dog for rabies, so the little girl had to undergo a series of six shots as a precaution. Needless to say, she wasn't every excited about it.

Kirk recalls, "The day she came into the hospital for her 5th shot, was my first time to treat her. When I brought the needle into the room she was trying to find a place to crawl her little body into, where I couldn't give her the shot. I calmed her down to the point where I was easily able to do it. I laughed when she said to me, *'Okay, when are you going to give me the shot?'* She didn't even feel it! That made me feel really good."

On Christmas Eve, the girl came back for her sixth and final shot. Kirk said, "She walked into the triage area and announced that only Mr. Spencer was going to give her the shot. No one else. Do you believe that? A five year old! They brought her to the pediatric unit and when I walked into the room, she already had her pants pulled down for me to give her the shot. I did it right away without so much as a word from her. She then gave me a big hug and took off."

Before leaving the hospital, the little girl had to see Dr. Marnie Rose, a very gifted and caring doctor in her own right. Kirk said, "Dr. Rose asked the little girl, *'Is it okay if Mr. Spencer gives me MY shots?'* Quickly, the girl's answer was NO! The five-year old then spread some Christmas cheer to the entire staff when she said, *'I'm the only one he can give a shot to, and if you don't like it, too bad!'"*

(Dr. Marnie Rose was also featured on *Houston Medical.* As a 28-year old, she battled a rare form of brain cancer that usually only strikes *men* twice her age. In an unexplainable case of bad things happening to good people, Marnie Rose's fight for life ended in August, 2002. Her loss is felt by many family, friends, and sick children in the Houston area.)

As for Kirk Spencer, he has no plans to ever change careers again. He is now back working at the Clear Lake Regional Medical Center where he worked before Hermann Memorial. It is much closer to his home and has nothing to do with the celebrity status he now enjoys since *Houston Medical.*

Kirk loves bonding with his own special guest stars, the sick little children he cares for with all of his heart. "Even if I hit the lottery, I would still go to work as a nurse," he says. They are the words of a man holding a daily winning ticket to a life filled with purpose.

When I asked Kirk if part of the reason he loves his job so much is because he is celebrating Greg, he got emotional before answering. "You're the first person who has ever asked me that. Thank you. Yes! I *am* celebrating Greg's life. He was a very special kid, and some of the things he could do were amazing. He just had a way of taking over a room and making everyone laugh. He could go to a park near where we lived and have squirrels and birds come to him, right into his hands! It was like St. Francis of Assisi. He definitely had a calmness about him.

What Greg had sits with me, and I want to continue him and his life. It ended way too soon. I don't want any parents or grandparents to go through what we did and I'll do anything to save a child's life. That's why I fight for every kid that I have as a patient."

Kirk Spencer has never had a patient die, although there have been a couple of close calls. "Knock on wood," he said. Perhaps, it's because he always knocks on heaven's door, asking for a little help with his sick little ones. "I feel like being a nurse is what I'm meant to do. I only wish I found it earlier in my life. This is where God wanted me to be and I enjoy every minute of it. It just took a long time for me to find it."

Special K's

Kiss a child every chance you get.

Steal kisses whenever necessary.

Savor every time a child offers you a kiss.

Keep an open heart with a child.

Keep an open mind with a child.

Keep your word with a child.

Hold keepsakes for a child.

Share knowledge with a child.

Teach a child that no one likes a "know-it-all."

Teach a child to knock before entering a room.

Play a game of kickball with a child.

Fly a kite with a child.

Sing karaoke with a child.

Allow a child to take karate lessons.

Let a child help in the kitchen.

Have a photo of a child on a key chain.

Give a child the key to your heart.

Give kudos to a child when they do something good.

Develop a knack of when to talk, and when to listen with a child.

Keep a never ending supply of kindness for a child.

"Why I Teach Children To Be Self-ish"

Kids report back to me that it never fails. One of my lessons always causes a stir among adults who don't hear it first-hand. Kids are told things about me like, "Don't listen to him! He's crazy!" I am guilty as charged because I do tell children it's okay to be "self-ish." (Notice I didn't write selfish, but rather *self-ish*.) I know why some parents initially react negatively. They only hear the headline from their children and rush to judgment before they hear what the "self-ish" lesson is really all about.

I make it clear to children that they *should* share with others. They *should* be kind to others. They *should* consider the feelings of others. They *should* treat others how they want to be treated themselves. I also tell children how I'm not worried about them being "brats" because I know none of them want to wear that label. I use the "self-ish" angle as an attention getter to make the point that I am really much more concerned about the growing number of children who do not like themselves, love themselves, or have healthy amounts of self-respect and self-esteem.

My *self-ish* point is to teach children to take care of "the self." I want them to learn what their needs are and how to get them met. I want them to have the courage to always ask for help when they need it. I want them to not only identify what feels good for them and right for them, but to also learn the things that hurt them and frighten them. Children who know how to take care of "the self" are the ones who steer clear of drugs, crime and other obstacles that lie in their path. Children who enjoy healthy relationships with themselves grow up to be the adults who enjoy success as spouses, parents, workers and friends.

I teach children to put themselves first. They understand if they take care of themselves, they are in a better position to be happy, confident and successful. They also learn that taking care of "the self" makes them much more able to help others do the same.

When kids tell their parents how some guy at school talked about being *selfish,* you can see how easily "buttons" can get pushed. Parents do understand and like my message once they hear it directly from me. Hopefully, you'll give it a chance too.

Baldrick's Books

Here is some of my favorite reading material for you to consider as part of your celebrations. This list features both books for kids and about kids:

ANYWAY, by Kent M. Keith

A CHILD CALLED IT, by Dave Pelzer

CHICKEN SOUP FOR THE KID'S SOUL, by Jack Canfield, Mark Victor Hansen

CHILDREN ARE FROM HEAVEN, John Gray, Ph.D.

CHILDREN'S LETTERS TO GOD, by Stuart Hample

CHOOSING UP SIDES, by John H. Ritter

GUESS HOW MUCH I LOVE YOU, by Sam McBratney

JOURNEY THROUGH HEARTSONGS, by Mattie J.T. Stepanek

KIDS RULE! The Hopes and Dreams of 21st Century Children, by Thomas Baldrick (You didn't think I'd leave it out, did you?)

THE ALCHEMIST, by Paulo Coehlo

THE GIVING TREE, by Shel Silverstein

the LITTLE SOUL and the SUN, by Neale Donald Walsch

Any book by Dr. Seuss

Any book by Lisa Funari-Willever

"The Beautiful Skye"

One of the greatest aspects of my work as an author is the opportunity to appear at schools. I am not yet a good enough writer to adequately describe the joy I feel from connecting with the students and caretakers at the schools I visit.

In a letter to the editor of *The Mercury*, a Pottstown, PA newspaper, I wrote, "If you come across my heart at the Royersford Elementary School, please let it be! If home is where the heart is, mine is surely there." I may eventually write countless pieces about how this suburban school celebrates children, but here's one story at the head of the class.

The night the first Harry Potter movie was released in November, 2001, was a magical evening indeed. While millions were excitedly filling theatres for what was then the most successful movie premiere ever, a couple hundred cautious and curious parents joined their kids at Royersford Elementary. The event was billed as a chance to see the results of the week long workshop I led as part of an author-in-residence program.

The week coming to an end had been one of the greatest of my life. I led students through teachings on finding their creativity and feeling their power. Fears were faced and hearts burst open from the love and life lessons I shared with the children.

A big hit with the kids was my message on the chalkboard, "Free Hugs! Just ask." I must have given and received a dozen hugs with each and every one of the 488 students. (A few times, kids were lined up 50 deep for hugs with me. I'm not kidding!) My back was convinced I had lifted four *million* and eighty-eight students, but I'm not complaining.

My talk to the packed gymnasium that night was very well-received. Many parents offered thanks, compliments and positive re-

Skylar DiGuiseppe getting the hug she wanted from Thomas.
Photo by King David Willauer.

views from their children regarding my visit. Time and again that night, I saw parents watch and wonder as their child asked me for yet another hug.

The families enjoyed how we transformed the school into an art gallery to showcase the creative work each student had done in recognizing a hero in their life.

Adults and children proudly roamed the halls lined with the priceless drawings and writings of the students. Each child's work was dedicated to a personal hero. (As a special surprise for the children, we invited all of the heroes. Many did attend.) The heroes honored were parents, grandparents, siblings, teachers, friends, police officers, firefighters and last but not least, even a certain author. Every hero left that night with a gift to last a lifetime. Some of us left with many gifts.

I was sure the highlight of the evening came when Principal Dave Willauer said this to the crowd about me, "He has changed the school forever." I was wrong. There were more highlights to come. It was nearly 9 o'clock at night, and time to see "The Beautiful Skye."

The long line in the school library where I was autographing books had finally come to an end. The principal, who I affectionately call, "King David" was sitting to my side at the table, acting as ambassador, fill-in cashier and friend. In walked one of my favorite little angels that week, a girl in the first grade named Skylar.

"Skye" is an adorable little one with whom I shared a number of hugs and smiles. With her in line was her mom, Nancy, the one who knew all too well about the lateness of "The Evening Skye," when she is up past her usual bedtime.

Between "King David" and me, I don't know who is more inclined to bring out the silliness in themselves and in children. Skye was definitely in on the gigglefest and her loving mom let it go on for a few minutes. We were telling Skye to look up the word "comedienne" in the dictionary. I also told her to look up "special" because I thought her picture should be in the dictionary right next to it.

I signed a book for Skye, and her mom took photos of us together. Nancy then made it quite clear that it was time to go home.

There was no doubt that mom was in charge and staying longer was not an issue for debate. But amazingly, Skye persisted.

The six-year old was respectful but persistent as she stood before her mother in front of the table where I was seated. Skye said, "No mom. We can't go yet." Her mom replied that she had seen enough. She even emphasized the name Skylar, to make the point. Nonetheless, Skye came back at her again. "We have to stay mom. This is important." Mom then announced the evening's end for what we all expected was the final time. Still, little Skylar stood firm, "I have to do this mom. This is important!"

The surprising showdown continued as Skye turned away from her mother and walked around the table to where I was seated. She then looked at me with the cutest puppy dog eyes and talked as if nothing had happened and no one else was around, "I have to go now," she said. "Can I have one more hug?" I looked at her stunned mother who immediately gave me the nod of approval. I then hugged this little girl like it was my final moment on earth. What an honor! I'm so grateful that King David grabbed a photo of the moment.

A month or so later, I received a Christmas card which I took as a sign that Santa Claus is alive and well. Nancy wrote, "*My daughter doesn't warm up to people easily, but when she hugged you goodbye and you scooped her in your arms, my heart was so full!*"

I wrote this story for a few reasons:

1. To point out how silly and hurtful we can be when we sell ourselves and others short. All day, I prepared myself for a poor turnout, thinking kids and parents would choose the Harry Potter movie over the school event.
2. To show that Skylar is proof of how children get the message to *ask* for what they need.
3. To remind you to treat every hug as though it may be your best or last.
4. I wrote this as a reminder so that whenever you have doubts about your own impact to make a difference in the life of a child, all you need to do is look toward "The Beautiful Skye."

Protect A Child As If Your Life Depends On It

Celebrate a child by keeping them healthy and safe.

Have plenty of Band-Aids and antiseptics ready.

Learn CPR.

Give a child daily vitamins.

Share a healthy diet with a child.

Have a child eat a healthy breakfast.

Limit a child's sugar intake.

Limit a child's "junk food" intake.

Prevent obesity.

Encourage a child to be active.

Only leave a child with a trusted babysitter.

Instill respect for the property of others.

Help a child to set healthy personal boundaries.

Teach a child self-defense.

Learn the Heimlich Maneuver.

Use sunscreen on a child.

Donate blood.

Be an organ donor.

Talk with a child about alcohol.

Don't abuse alcohol.

Don't drink and drive.

Talk with a child about drugs.

Don't abuse drugs.

Pay attention to a child's sudden changes in behavior.

Don't smoke.

Teach a child not to smoke.

Take a child for medical checkups regularly.

Take a child for dental checkups regularly.

Drive carefully.

Always wear seatbelts.

Always use car seats with little ones.

Install a home alarm system.

Have working smoke alarms at home.

Have fire drills at home.

Teach a child respect for fire.

Childproof your home as best you can.

Keep firearms away from a child.

Teach a child that violence is unacceptable.

Hit a child ONLY where you like to be hit.

Teach a child an emergency response plan that includes dialing 9-1-1.

Teach a child how to swim.

Never leave a small child unattended at a pool.

Have a last will and testament.

Sports Shorts

In my mind, many people come up short in dealing with sports. Why do most kids play sports anyway? To win trophies? I hope not. To win multi-million dollar contracts? I hope not. Championships and visions of super-stardom are often far more important to the adults in little league than the children who play the games. Please don't make these issues for a child.

Kids want to have fun. Sports can be fun. Kids want to feel a part of something, a team, a sense of community. Sports provide those opportunities. Kids want to excel at whatever they do, but let's face it, not all are destined to be great athletes.

Too many little league coaches seem to act like a frustrated sports TV junkie or a wanna-be Phil Jackson or Joe Torre. I've also seen kids who are so nervous about performing up to the expectations of grownups, that having fun is nearly as impossible for them as becoming the next Kobe Bryant!

Here are some ideas for celebrating a child and making sports fun:

Turn the sound off while watching a game on TV, and you be the announcers!

Lift a child high enough to dunk a basketball.

Take a child to a big-time professional game.

Take a child to a minor league game.

Hang out before or after a game for a child to get autographs.

Take a child to watch a game at your alma mater.

Take a child to see the Harlem Globetrotters.

Shoot pool as a team.

Play doubles tennis.

Hit golf balls at a driving range.

Play a round of miniature golf.

Have a tailgate party.

Become a "kid-friendly" little league coach.

Teach a child to respect their opponents.

Teach a child how to win with grace.

Teach a child how lose with dignity.

Teach a child that "winning at all costs" is expensive.

Congratulate a child for doing their best at sports.

Practice sports with a child.

Make a child feel like a winner.

Thomas with "good sports," Elmo, Zoey, and Make-A-Wish kids, Steven and Erica Mannella, at Sesame Place.

Little Things To You Can Be Big Things To Little Ones

Take a fresh look at things we forget, disregard as trivial, or consider speed bumps to our busy pace. They can be SO BIG to a little person.

Playing in a large empty box.

Receiving mail.

Placing letters in a slot or mailbox.

Using chalk on the driveway or sidewalk.

Using water paints.

Licking the icing off utensils when baking a cake.

Pushing the button for your floor on an elevator.

Riding in a see-through elevator.

Let a child give their meal order to a restaurant server.

Let a child talk at a drive-thru window.

Display a child's artwork on the refrigerator.

Teach a child how to wink.

Teach a child how to whistle.

Videotape, photograph, and keep records of a child's "firsts" and other accomplishments. You'll all appreciate it years later.

Keep a growth chart of a child.

Let a child have sleepover parties.

Always introduce a child when meeting others.

Remember "Quality Time" is a fairy tale believed only by adults.

Honor and respect a child's attachments to worldly possessions instead of throwing things out without asking.

Making Time For Madeline

It was by no means a leisurely winter Sunday. I worked so busily at my computer all morning that I never even made it to the gym for my intended workout. I wasn't all that interested in watching the St. Louis Rams predicted win over the New England Patriots later on in the 2002 Super Bowl. The highlight of my day would be watching my nephew Matthew blow out the candles on the cake at his third birthday party.

Though I never played in the NFL, I covered the league for years as a TV producer and reporter. Therefore, I had a good idea of what it felt like to lose on Super Bowl Sunday. Now, out of nowhere, I was facing the agony of defeat on the big day, and there was little I could do about it.

Boom! It hit with the impact of John Madden yelling in my ear. I had committed a fumble all right, and had no excuse. The hands on the clock were clenched like fists in my face. I was not worried about missing any of the game or the start of the birthday party for that matter. Suddenly, I was sick over the thought of failing to keep my word with another precious little one I adore.

Earlier in the week, I was talking on the telephone with Matthew's older sister, Madeline. At four-years old, the responsibilities of a big sister are not always easy. Nor, are they always easily embraced. I knew all the attention and presents Matthew would receive on his birthday, would at times be hard for Madeline to accept. So, I promised her that Uncle Tommy would arrive early on Sunday so that she and I would have play time together, before all of the party guests arrived.

Since she is more like age four going on twenty-four, Madeline instructed me to come to the house during her nap. She told me that Matthew and her little sister Lauren, take longer naps than

Three sources of joy to the world ... Madeline, her little brother, Matthew, and little sister, Lauren.

she does. Therefore, it would mean playtime for just the two of us. I didn't merely agree with Madeline. No, I promised her I would be there when she rose from her nap.

Panic set in as I jumped into action. I changed clothes, wrapped Matthew's presents, and left my house as though it were on fire. I sped away, planning to shorten a forty-five minute drive by taking a few liberties with the speed limit. I would not do anything to risk someone getting hurt, but I did ask the traffic Gods to grant my last-minute plea for protection and a free pass from all radar guns.

I didn't listen to the radio or cd player. My choice had nothing to do with distracting me from driving. I simply realized that even at maximum volume, my sound system could not quiet the inner voices that were feasting on my futility. How could I be so stupid? How could I possibly be in position to break a promise to a little girl I love so dearly? What kind of a hypocrite child advocate was I, that I could put work before her little feelings?

I did use my cell phone to call Maddie's daddy. I told him exactly what was going on. He calmly told me not to worry about it. He said Madeline was excited that I was coming early, but that she would understand. I disagreed, probably because even I didn't understand.

The traffic Gods must not work as a skeleton crew on the weekends. On my drive, I seemed to make every light and had very few motorists (especially no police cars) as obstacles. When I exited the highway, I felt there still was a chance I would reach the house before Madeline awoke. It was then that I found a slow moving vehicle directly in front of me.

The vehicle was big and yellow with plenty of lights, signs, windows and passengers. It even had a rear door. You guessed right. Somehow, on a Sunday, Super Bowl Sunday no less, I found myself behind a school bus on a two lane road! I couldn't believe it. Knowing this was no accident, I just sat there and laughed.

Everything happens for a reason, even when you don't like the reasons. Like it or not, I was slowed down. Like it or not, I would get to Madeline's house when I got there. Not a moment before. Like it or not, it was just as it says in the arcade: Race Ended.

As I waited at the red light, a couple of children looked at me from the back window of the bus. I waved to them and they waved back. Life was different now. My stress and anxiety were gone. I chose happiness and calmness as replacements. I tossed a big smile at what was now a bigger group of children. They were smiling at me as even more kids joined in. I then began to make funny faces and they did the same. We all shared laughs as the light turned green.

I was living fully in the moment. The time I had so little of before, now seemed to stand still. The silliness with the children escalated and lasted for a few blocks until my scheduled turn appeared. But, before I made my right, I pulled along side of the bus, honking my horn and waving out the window. The children were laughing and loving it!

There were only a couple miles remaining as I reached the hilly and narrow winding roads portion of my trip. I could still not go fast. Sadly but calmly, I began to prepare to disappoint myself and Madeline. A sincere apology was the best I could do.

Amazingly, Madeline's nap that afternoon was longer than usual. I made the mistake of never even considering that as a possibility. Into the house I ran, only to wait five minutes before she awoke. She came downstairs calling for her Uncle Tommy, and was so happy to see me there. We played non-stop outside in the cold until the party began, and sweet Maddie Jane was a champion big sister all-day.

I wrote about this snatching of a Super Bowl Sunday victory from the jaws of defeat, not to give myself a trophy for getting there in time. I made a number of wrong choices that day and was extremely lucky in the outcome. I chose to tell this tale was because it offered so many valuable lessons in celebrating a child. Such as:

> Remember, children remember promises we make to them.
>
> Never make a promise to a child, you're not able to keep.
>
> Give love and attention to the siblings of a birthday boy or girl. They will appreciate it more than you may think.
>
> Know (especially on weekends) that work will *always* be there.
>
> Never be in such a hurry that you lose sight of what you find to be truly important.
>
> Live life "in the now" as a collection of moments. Otherwise, you miss so many of them.
>
> Always be careful and patient with a school bus.
>
> Always remember the joy you can create by simply waving to kids on a school bus!
>
> Teach a child (and yourself) time management.

They Want The Truth. They CAN Handle The Truth

It's never impossible for any of us to "right a wrong," no matter how long ago it happened. Recently, I heard a story of an old man who anonymously mailed payment of $100 to his alma mater more than 50 years after he graduated. It turns out the man wrote an apology and wanted to free himself of the guilt he was carrying over stealing some minor items when he was a student at the school.

While we can't change the results of the sad but true events that have taken place in our own lives or in the world, we can create new results. We can teach a child right from wrong. We can teach a child that all people, races, colors, or genders are not the same. They are different, and that's okay. If we all looked the same, sounded the same, and were the same, the world would be a very boring place.

When a child is old enough, please talk with him or her about some of the sad but true realities of the past and present. If you do this, you will be doing your part to ensure they don't happen in the future.

Teach a child about the horror of Hitler and the Holocaust.

Teach a child about the cruelty of slavery.

Teach a child about the notorious treatment of our Native Americans.

Teach a child about the ignorance of the Ku Klux Klan.

Teach a child that blood can be more important than skin. After all, we all bleed the same color.

Teach a child to respect all religions.

Teach a child that prejudice is not related to common sense.

Teach a child to make room in their heart for the perils of the homeless.

Watch The History Channel with a child.

Child ... You Need Some Thankful Therapy

Ursela Mangum is in the business of caring. She is founder of Mother to Mother www.mothertomothersupport.com, a company offering birth and postpartum support services for mothers and their families. I recognize that helping mommys, daddys, big brothers and big sisters adjust to the arrival of a newborn, are undeniable celebrations of children. However, this story celebrates Ursela's seeing through the thick clouds covering the relationship she shares with the oldest of her own two children.

As an expectant mother for the first time, Ursela was able to track the stormy relationship with her child, much in the way meteorologists follow looming hurricanes. Long before the public sees the heavy wind and rain reach landfall, the experts watch the storm's effect at sea. Ursela did the same thing with her son, Ean, early on while he was still in the womb.

She and her loving husband, Glenn, stuck it out through her morning sickness, food cravings, pre-term labor, and over 22 hours of excruciating labor. Once the eye of the hurricane passed, and baby Ean was born, there were plenty of late-night nursings, as well as feelings of isolation and loneliness for Ursela, a sudden "stay at home" mom.

Years later, this woman who describes herself as a "typical neurotic mom," remains optimistic, even though she is waiting on a sunny day more often than not. Her now seven-year old son, Ean, is "a high maintenance child," she says. "Sometimes he has good days, but he whines and complains almost daily. Ean is emotionally driven in so many different ways, with very high highs and very low lows."

So you see, even a highly trained professional experienced in family therapy, crisis intervention, and consulting for mothers, can have her own parenting challenges. Ursela loves her son and knows Ean loves her, too. "He's an easy one to say I love you mommy. But, it's also easy for him to let me know when he doesn't like me," she laughs.

Ursela recognized she was allowing Ean's constant complaining to drag her down. "I found myself raising my voice too often and knew I needed a change," she admitted. (Author's note: Let's celebrate that Ursela said *she* needed a change and simply didn't blame the boy.)

Over a year ago, there came a day when Ean emerged as such a cranky little camper that his mother felt they had reached a crossroads. "In a manic mommy's moment, I just decided that I was going to kill him with kindness," she said. "I told him, Ean, what you need to do is stop complaining and take a dose of some Thankful Therapy! He then gave me this look like, what is this crazy woman talking about?"

Right then, while driving her son to kindergarten, Ursela came upon a way to stop his whining. The idea was to make the five-year old say five things he was grateful for in his life. "I didn't really want to do it," claims Ean.

He spoke of things like having school that day, being able to play, and having friends he could play with. It worked. "I then decided we would take five minutes out of every day to refocus Ean on the positive things in his life," says Ursela.

Though by no means a miracle cure that has broken the boy's habit of complaining, it has given her family a break. "Most of the time, I now pick things that are obvious," said Ean. "I want to have a nice day at school. I hope I am going to make new friends." Every morning, as they put on their seat belts, (another cause for celebration), Ean and Ursela take turns expressing their gratitude. He says, "Me and my mom don't get to spend a lot of time together. She works and I'm in school. So, doing this has made me very, very happy."

Sometimes Ean's three-year old sister, Kalena, does it, too. "My little sister, she's wild. She sometimes scratches, bites, licks and pushes. Most of the time I just tell on her because I don't like when she does that."

Ean prefers the Thankful Therapy is just he and his mom. He doesn't do it with his dad, only his mom. It is a daily ritual they never forget. Ursela says, "It works for me too, because sometimes I am in a bad mood. My son and I have such a tumultuous relationship. There's love, anger, frustration, and happiness. Yet, I have found I live for those moments of thankfulness."

On the good mornings, Ursela savors hearing her son say things like, "I'm *really* grateful my mommy came home from her business trip." He claims, "I feel a lot better doing this because I've been nice to God and have made new friends at school."

However, there are the tougher mornings when Ean is not happy about brushing his teeth or much else. He'll say his thankful things begrudgingly, with offerings such as, "I'm thankful I woke up this morning." (Author's note: Be honest. We've all been there.)

Ursela believes there have been a handful of mornings when she and Ean faced other crossroads situations in their relationship. At those times, she says Ean tests her with looks of defiance, and threats of not doing their Thankful Therapy session. "On those mornings, I'll tell Ean that maybe he can write it down later. Or, maybe when he comes home he'll feel thankful. But, he always breaks down and says, 'Okay. Fine. I'm grateful for…' and goes right through his five things. If you can watch it from the outside, it's really quite amusing," says Ursela.

Another source of enjoyment for Ean's mom is the effect Thankful Therapy has had on him. "Each day, I'm waiting to hear what growth there is in him. It breaks through some days. He may not notice it, but I do. I've noticed what he is thankful for has grown deeper," observes Ursela. "Ean can now say things like, 'I'm thankful I woke up in a good mood this morning. I'm thankful my mommy and daddy love me. I'm thankful my daddy is going to take me to soccer practice.' It's wonderful," she says. Ean adds, "The most things I've ever been thankful for in one day is 15. Mainly, it's hard to get to five because I like to say the same things."

There is no such thing as a fine whine. Whining does not get better with age, and is not the sound of music to anyone's ears I know. Therefore, I celebrate this mommy for staying tuned in and finding something that works to help both her and her son. It certainly must be trying to have a young child whose view of the world has always seemed to be that the sippy cup is half-empty instead of half-full.

Ursela wants others to know what the "Thankful Therapy" means to her. "It's Mommy Time Out time, but Ean and I are not separated or isolated from each other. It brings us together and we're interacting. I know there will be times that Ean will smile when he looks back on it. He may complain to his friends about doing our Thankful Therapy, but I do believe he will remember it as times we shared together. I want it to bring him happiness for many years to come."

The feeling is mutual. Ean says, "I want to do my thankful therapy with my mom until I'm 92, if I ever live that long." When I pointed out to Ean that his mom would have to live to a much older age than that in order to keep doing it with him, he replied, "Whenever I ask my mom how old she is, she keeps on saying she's only 29. So, that's a mystery to me."

Sticking Themselves, Sticking Together

In 1620, a party of pilgrims from the Mayflower first stepped ashore this great land of ours at Plymouth Rock. Nearly 400 years later in the same spot of Plymouth, Massachusetts, there lives another brave pilgrim quite worthy of celebration.

The sacred journey of seven-year old Lauren McCarthy did not involve sailing across the Atlantic Ocean. It did not take her beyond the town limits either. In truth, the powerful pilgrimage of this little girl did not even require her to go past the end of the street where her family lives. It is the destination not the distance that is important here folks. "Kids just rise to the occasion," Lauren's mother, Moira, says proudly.

Before taking you on Lauren's journey, I must first give you an idea of its origin. During kindergarten, Lauren was diagnosed with Juvenile Diabetes after she nearly slipped into a coma. The doctor told the McCarthy's, "If any family can handle this, it's yours." No parents ever want to hear those kinds of compliments. (I also have to celebrate Lauren for something at that time. While lying in a hospital bed, the kindergartner told a nurse, "Please don't talk like I'm not here! This is about ME! Tell me what I need to know!" Thanks for teaching, Lauren!)

While I cannot find a cure for Juvenile Diabetes with this story, I can give it a much needed facelift. You see, one of the problems in battling this chronic disease affecting 17 million Americans, is that to others, a child like Lauren appears to be healthy and heavenly, when in fact; she and her family knows her life is a living hell.

Juvenile Diabetes is something a child never outgrows. Another 35 American children are newly diagnosed every day. It turns children into physical and emotional prisoners in their own bodies. To stay alive, children need to give the disease constant attention by pricking their little fingers for blood sugar tests. They must also take insulin injections to do for the body what the pancreas won't. Children like Lauren with Juvenile Diabetes are sticking themselves with an average of thirteen needles per day. I have yet to meet a child who likes getting one needle once in a while. And I've been around an awful lot of sick kids.

"No matter how used to it we get, no matter how smart Lauren is about her care, this is no way for her to live," cries her mother. "Lauren doesn't complain, but she should. Her fingers are raw. She worries about her future, asking me things like, 'Mommy, can I have kids? Do you promise I can?' She should just be a silly little girl."

Actress Mary Tyler Moore, Chairperson of the Juvenile Diabetes Research Foundation www.jdrf.org, puts it this way, "I've had juvenile diabetes for over 30 years. It changes everything about a person's life. And to add to the day-in, day-out hassles of living with diabetes—the balancing of diet, exercise, and insulin, the shots, the terrible episodes of low blood sugar, the weird feelings of high blood sugar—is the knowledge that even if you do all you can do to be as normal as possible, you're not, you're different, and you face the uncertainty of a life visited upon by early death, blindness, kidney failure, amputation, heart attack, or stroke."

So, now you know. Now, you have a sense of what little Lauren McCarthy knew when she began her sacred journey. In second grade, she was in a class by herself at her school of 700 students. Lauren had been the only diabetic child.

One day, Moira McCarthy received a telephone call from a neighbor that another girl on their street had just been diagnosed with Juvenile Diabetes. The girl was the same age as Lauren. They were not enemies, but they had never really connected as friends either.

"After getting dismissed from school, my mom said there was something she wanted to tell me," recalls Lauren. "She told me that Jaclyn had Juvenile Diabetes. I was sad. I thought it was a strange coincidence."

"It was one of those moments you never forget," says Moira, "When I told Lauren, her knees literally buckled under her with the weight of what that meant. She fell to the ground. It was like someone knocked the wind out of her." Lauren remembers, too. "I was really sad. I knew that Jaclyn would have to do all the stuff that I did. I knew how hard it was, and I didn't want her to have to do that."

Moira says when Lauren pulled herself together, "She looked me right in the eye and said, 'Oh, Mommy, we have to help her.' Lauren adds, "I knew I could teach Jaclyn how to do shots, and my mom could teach her mom how to try insulin and what numbers were good or bad."

Moira explained to her daughter that just because Jaclyn now had diabetes, too, it didn't mean she had to suddenly like her. Lauren immediately corrected her. "She told me, 'She's like a sister now, mom. You wouldn't understand it, but she is.'

Actually, Lauren's mother did understand. "It was a really good lesson for me," she says. "Lauren showed that you just have to do the right thing. The immediacy of her decision was very impressive. Knocking the wind out of her really showed me the profound effect diabetes had on her. The impact was unbelievable. I wasn't in denial then. I saw how deeply she felt the pain, emotionally, physically, and mentally. Lauren knew she had the unique ability to give this girl the help she needed."

And so, immediately after Jaclyn arrived home from the hospital, little Lauren McCarthy embarked on her truly sacred journey. The pilgrimage took less than a minute, as she walked two houses down from her own to embrace and console Jaclyn.

"Lauren bought her a caboodle just like hers," says Moira. "Little girls usually keep makeup in them, but we found it was an interesting and less scary way to store things such as syringes, alcohol, and swabs." Lauren says Jaclyn liked the gift and the support. "She said it made it easier, and she really liked having a new friend who had Juvenile Diabetes. We saw each other differently. We then looked out and cared for each other."

Three years later, Lauren and Jaclyn are separated by distance since Jaclyn's family moved down south. Lauren was named as a delegate to represent her state at the JDRF Children's Congress in Washington, D.C. The president and the U.S. Congress are listening to the JDRF children, and are providing increases in federal funding for research.

Moira McCarthy volunteers as the President of the Bay State Chapter of JDRF. I celebrate the organization founded by caring parents who joined together in their dedication to finding a cure. There are definite signs of progress with advancements in maintenance such as the insulin pump and treatments such as Islet Transplantation. This exciting procedure takes insulin-producing beta cells from a donor's pancreas and transfers them to a person with diabetes. (I have personally met Jody DeMarco, one of the first successful transplant recipients. She is insulin free!)

I've been a speaker at functions for the JDRF Greater Delaware Valley Chapter, with another girl named Ashley Bree. She is a teenage advocate who was diagnosed with diabetes at age two. In an average year, Ashley states that she pricks her finger for blood sugar testing over 2100 times. She also used to be on the receiving end of over 1000 insulin shots a year.

Ashley says, "Since I started on the insulin pump, now the fun comes every other evening. That is when I remove the catheter in my stomach to change the pump reservoir and tubing. I then insert a new catheter into my stomach using a long, sharp pointy needle which I may add, stings."

Ashley says when her blood sugar is high, she is thirsty, snappy, and can't think clearly. When it's low, she feels shaky and whiny. In either case, Ashley is a master of summing up diabetes in a few words when she says, 'Excuse my language but, *it sucks!"* When I shared Ashley's description with Lauren McCarthy, she sheepishly said, "I'd have to say the same as her."

There is hope for a cure. There is hope for the future of mankind thanks to stories like this of children helping children. Even though it is harder than we'll ever know, children like Lauren and Ashley are sticking themselves and sticking together.

Nurture Nature

Teach a child to nurture nature and have respect for it. Try these activities and lessons to celebrate the great outdoors with a child.

Lay on the ground and look up at the sky.

Gaze at the stars.

Wish upon the stars.

Look through a telescope.

Visit an aquarium.

Visit an observatory.

Visit a planetarium.

Teach a child to conserve energy.

Watch a sunrise.

Watch a sunset.

Do gardening.

Pick apples.

Pick pumpkins.

Go canoeing.

Go boating.

Go sailing.

Go kayaking.

Go on a picnic.

Go hiking.

Take a drive in a convertible.

Go camping.

Take a child to the circus.

Teach a child the "do's and don'ts" around doggies and other animals.

Catch and release insects such as lightning bugs.

Go birdwatching.

Go on a whalewatching boat.

Do a swim with the dolphins session.

Show a child how to skim rocks across water.

Take a ferry ride.

Walk the beach.

Go horseback riding.

Go bike riding.

Share an umbrella.

Visit a rain forest.

Visit the U.S. National Parks.

Visit an active volcano.

Build a snowman.

Have a snowball fight.

Lay on the ground and make snow angels.

Watch and listen to falling snow.

Teach a child never to litter.

Oh, Those Pied Piepers!

What a memorable date it was for Marianne and Blaine. Hey now! The date wasn't marked by a burst of fireworks from their first romantic kiss. Blaine didn't get down on one knee either. In reality, it was much too late for those kinds of milestones in their relationship.

When they went on this date early in 1994, Blaine and Marianne were already "Mr. and Mrs. Pieper (pronounced piper)." They also had five little Piepers running around the house. (We should celebrate this husband and wife for recognizing the importance of spending time as a couple. Devoting time to enjoy each other on dates sends a great message to their kids. It also helps to keep Marianne and Blaine happier as spouses, and parents, too.)

The buildup for the much-ballyhooed date was not due to anything the Piepers did that night, but rather something they said they would do. During conversation at dinner, Marianne and Blaine came up with the one idea that has since had many of the residents of Ohio County, Kentucky saying, *"Oh, those Pied Piepers!"*

Marianne recalls, "We were talking about our five children, and how kids in general often feel they are not important or appreciated. But adults do care. It's just not communicated very well because we don't take the time. We're all just so busy."

The Piepers decided they would take the time to create a "Celebrate the Child" event. As a volunteer mom, Marianne was the original driving force. Meanwhile, as a hospital administrator, Blaine got his employer to be one of the sponsors. "Sometimes, there's just a natural order to things," said Marianne. "Other people immediately took to the idea."

Ohio County is the fifth largest in Kentucky, but doesn't have many people to brag about it. The county sits quietly southwest of Louisville, between Owensboro and Bowling Green, with a popula-

A little boy being celebrated in Ohio County, KY.

tion just north of 20,000. "It's a rural community. Most people work in agriculture and education. And it does have a Perdue factory," says Gary Druin, a local 4-H agent.

Judy Burns, of the University of Kentucky Cooperative Extension Service adds, "Over 50% of the kids in our grade schools live in poverty. Unfortunately, the rate is even higher for pre-schoolers." Is there something wrong with me, or does Ohio County not seem like it has the blueprint for a successful children's event in the Blue Grass State?

Regardless, the first Celebrate the Child Day was held in April 1994 at the county middle school. It featured games for the children and helpful information for parents. A little more than 300 people attended. "I guess we thought we hit the gold mine," laughs Gary Druin, "and we didn't even fill the gym."

Dee Donlon, coordinator of the Western Elementary Family Resource Center, also laughs about the humble beginnings. "I was treasurer for three years of Celebrate the Child, and never wrote a check! We sent out letters and got only $55 in donations, although some businesses did pay for certain bills," he said.

The Celebrate the Child Day in Ohio County made it to an annual event because a few hard-working people cared enough about children to keep it going. "We did it to help prevent drug and alcohol abuse with our youth," says Marianne Pieper. "Ohio County is a dry county, but it's the same as anywhere else because kids are still able to find things if they want them. So, we built our event around the forty developmental assets that the Search Institute has identified as being critical for shaping children's lives." www.search-institute.org

A big part of Celebrate the Child is the featured section called "Asset Alley." Kids play games that teach them about a particular asset, while the parents get taught separately about the assets in a totally non-threatening way. "It's reaching all different kinds of families. We know we're getting to those who really need help with their parenting. I think that's what gives us the strength to go on," says Marianne. "These aren't people who are likely to come to a parenting class where they feel they will be scrutinized. But, they'll come here for a day of fun and know they will leave having learned something valuable."

After a few years of celebrations, a big gift came when the newly formed school-community coalition, Together We Care, cared enough about the event to adopt it. Across Ohio County, it created a team of businesses and organizations. Together they do care. They work as one to improve the quality of life for children.

By the 10th Celebrate the Child event, it was forced to move to the high school because the annual attendance had grown to more than 4,000. If that doesn't seem like much to you, look at it as Marianne does, "We've got nearly one quarter of the people who are spread out for miles across our county, coming together one day a year to say, 'Kids are important. We value you.' It surprises me very much. Though I'm certainly happy about it," she said. Few communities can claim such success.

Cindy Fulton moved her family from Chicago to Ohio County just prior to the inaugural Celebrate the Child event. The Fultons have yet to miss a year. "There's so much stuff, so much helpful information, and so many activities for the kids. There are shows to enjoy, and chances for the children to showcase their little talents," says Cindy. "The day always makes me appreciate my kids even more, and also the county where we live and how we all pull together."

12-year old Sarah Fulton likes the event, and says it really helps. "Grownups just don't have enough time for us in between work, running errands, and paying bills. That makes us feel kind of left out. Celebrate the Child shows that the people who go there really appreciate children and are not selfish," she says. "I notice parents don't just drop off the kids. They stay with their children. They're not wasting all their time at work. They go there to have fun."

Basically everything except food is still free, making it a true celebration of children, and not a *Sell-a-bration* "with folks making money off our poor community," says Judy Burns. Still on a shoestring budget without advertising, the event now gets funded by roughly 75 local businesses and organizations, most of which ask if they can be involved.

Hundreds of volunteers, including a youth advisory committee do much of the work year after year. "The kids often save the day," admits Marianne Pieper. "If we are going to do something stupid, they tell us. They're just a whole lot cooler than we are," she laughs. "Once you've been to Celebrate the Child, you don't ever want to not be a part of it," says Judy Burns. "To see the sparkle in the kids' eyes, you can't even measure the difference you make. It's the best thing we do in this county."

Celebrate the Child is not a one day wonder. It has changed the feel of the community and created one movement. "They say it takes a village to raise a child, and that's what we're doing. Everybody is working together in one proud community," says Gary Druin. As a 4-H agent, he typifies what the outstanding organization has been doing for more than a century. "Youth development, working with kids, cows, cooking, community service. You name it. I do it," he says.

Ohio County now has a mentoring program in which businesses give time off to more than 100 employees to celebrate local children and guide them toward greatness. Adults of all ages are trying to improve their relationships with the boys who bag their groceries, and the girls who live in their neighborhood. Kids wear Celebrate the Child T-shirts with pride. Many of them are already young givers to society, doing a tremendous amount of community service across the county.

Judy Burns offers a wonderful example of how this agricultural community is growing a great crop of tomorrow's leaders. She received a telephone call from a young girl she mentored a few years ago, but had not seen because the girl's family moved. As soon as the girl heard Judy had surgery to repair a torn rotator cuff, she called to wish her well. Judy boasts, "I couldn't have been any more thrilled than if the president himself called me."

I hope this story will prevent people from having negative perceptions of rural communities. I wrote about Celebrate the Child hoping others would like the idea so much, they'd want to do something similar for the children in their own community. Ohio County would be happy to help any group who wants to follow their "Pied Piepers" in celebrating a child. For more information, log on to www.ohio.k12.ky.us/togetherwecare for more information.

Gary Druin said, "Our small town spirit proves that bigger isn't always better." If you still haven't been convinced, I'll leave you with one final point. The Ohio County Celebrate the Child Day is so great . . . even kids of all ages aren't embarrassed by it! Sarah Fulton explains, "Kids don't worry about being seen with their family because they're proud to have them there. Kids appreciate being with their parents, and the parents appreciate being with their kids."

Now that is some big-time magic in a small town setting, quite worthy of celebration.

Maybe She Is Able To Leap Tall Buildings In A Single Bound

I know she is faster than a speeding bullet. I know she is more powerful than a locomotive. I also know this celebration of Kassandra Guymon is likely to give you chills from head to toe. I know about the chills all too well because I get them every time I share the story with someone. (It often brings me to tears, too.)

This is not one of those stories about adrenalin helping someone to lift a car off an injured person. It's even more amazing than that.

It was a Wednesday morning in March in rural Clinton, Utah, north of Salt Lake City. At the Guymon house, it was not just Wednesday morning, but a really wacky Wednesday morning. "Every thing that could possibly go wrong, went wrong," laughs Kassandra.

Normally, the high school senior and oldest of five children would drive to school with her father because his workplace was next door to her school. However, on this particular morning, the seniors were given a later start because the lower grades were being tested.

A crisis for Kassandra came as she was getting ready for school. The family dryer had broken. She would not be able to wear the shirt she had her heart set on wearing. The shirt was wet. She was hot about it.

Next, as Kassandra was already running late in the hopes of being driven to meet the school bus, her mother Katherine forgot something and had to run back into the locked house. Perfect! This allowed just enough time for Kassandra's youngest brother Brock, an unusually obedient three-year old, to slip on the one piece of snow in the front yard that the warm weather hadn't melted. It sent him on an all-expense paid full body trip into the mud he was specifically told to avoid.

After a quick clean up of Brock, if the planets were aligned, the winds were at their backs, and the roads deserted, there might still be a chance for Kassandra to make it to the bus stop in time. Who knows? Maybe the bus driver was having a tough morning, too. It was worth a chance. If not, the Guymons would have to make the long drive to Northridge High.

"I never go straight east because of the railroad tracks," says Katherine. "I don't have time to get stuck and wait for the trains crossing. But, the weirdest thing is that morning; I drove right past the overpass turn. I knew it was a really stupid thing. I could have easily turned around, but for some reason I kept going straight."

Encountering no more difficulties, the Guymons reached the busy stretch of road linking Clinton to the town of Sunset. There, they came upon the railroad crossing that Katherine had always avoided. Yes! There was no train crossing!

The morning's bad luck would soon be over once they met the school bus. Katherine could proceed driving on her merry way right across the railroad tracks. But she didn't.

"As we were passing, I slowed down because I saw a little boy alone on the railroad tracks with his bike nearby," says Katherine. As a loving mother of five, she could not ignore a four-year old in this situation, no matter how happy she could see he was at the time. "He actually turned around and looked right at us," added Kassandra. "Hundreds of cars must have driven past him, but we were the only ones who stopped."

There wasn't a train in sight, but Katherine turned their car around anyway. She says, "A voice said to me, 'stop! Teach your child. Don't tell her what to do here. Teach!' I know I shouldn't have, but I stopped dead on the tracks. I asked Kassandra, 'what do you think? Take a really close look at this boy. Does this seem normal to you?' She said, 'No.' I then asked, 'and do you think he'll move if a train comes?' She again answered, 'no.' 'So what's the right thing to do here?' I asked. Kassandra said, 'We have to help.' I then pulled over onto a little street on the Clinton side of the tracks and asked her to go get him."

"At first I was just going to ask the boy if his mom knew where he was," claims Kassandra. "But I didn't want anyone to think we

Kassandra Guymon at the scene of the miracle.
Photo by: Alan Murray. Courtesy of *The Standard-Examiner*.

were trying to kidnap him. My mom then shouted to me to go knock on the door at the nearest house." So much for that idea, the man at the house about a half block away answered, but spoke only Spanish. Kassandra did not.

She says, "While I was trying to talk to the man, I saw the gates go down at the intersection and the horn started to blare." "All of a sudden, I could see the top of the train coming," says her mother. "I could clearly see the boy was excited. His face just lit up. He was so happy. There he was in the middle of the tracks, jumping up and down and waving his little arms." The four-year old who loved trains had no clue that the very thing he was waiting for was only seconds away from ending his life.

Kassandra says, "Mom screamed, 'the train is coming! Get him Kassandra!' But I could no longer see exactly where the boy was." Both describe what happened next as "incredibly spiritual."

Kassandra took off running IN SANDALS! "When I started I could see I was the same distance away as the train," she says. "I had so much adrenalin. All I could think about was getting that boy off the tracks," she says. "I got slowed down because I kicked off my sandals in the middle of the street."

At that point, her mother Katherine could not believe her eyes. "When Kassandra got out of her click-clock shoes. She ran faster than I have ever seen a human being run. Ever. It was faster than Olympic speed, I swear. Kassandra got there, lifted the boy in her arms and moved backwards," says Katherine. "I was numb. I thought I just sacrificed my daughter for a stranger's small child."

"My mom thought I hadn't pulled him away," says Kassandra. "It wasn't seconds before the train passed us. It was fragments of a second. We were half an arm's length away when I realized, 'oh my gosh! I'm right next to a massive train!' That was really intimidating and way too close for me."

Unfrozen, Katherine saw her daughter and ran up to her. "She had knelt down right next to the tracks and was holding the boy in her arms." Kassandra admits, "He didn't comprehend that he was in any kind of danger. He was actually more afraid of me than the train. He had been there waiting for the engineer."

A Sunset Police officer was near the back of the line in traffic. He was able to restore order before what happened had really registered with Kassandra. "Maybe about 45 minutes later it hit me. I realized I had been on the tracks, too! I did talk to the conductor. He told me that it was a miracle. He saw the little boy was going to die. He saw my life flash before his eyes, too. He thanked me because I saved so many people like him from the horror of watching it happen."

Though it's not something anyone would like, one can understand how a four-year old boy's fascination with trains could get him into trouble. What is much harder to explain is how a 17-year old girl who was never a school athlete, who jogs but doesn't consider herself to be fast, could outrun a speeding train . . . especially starting out IN SANDALS!

In their search for answers, both Kassandra and Katherine arrive at the "A" word. Granted, an adrenalin rush was involved. I mean the other "A" word. "There had to be angels involved," says Kassandra. "It's impossible for a 1500-ton train to stop or slow down in half a block. Maybe a higher being helped me out. I do know I couldn't have done it on my own." Her mother has a similar belief. "I really do think angels held back that train because no human being can run faster than a speeding train. There is a reason for both of them to be here."

Before you go rushing to judgment about the boy's family situation, allow Katherine and Kassandra to explain. "Soon after it happened, a woman picked up the boy and the bike. She was clearly shaken. I mean she was really freaked. She was walking weird," says Katherine.

Kassandra says she talked with her. It was the boy's mother. "They lived within three blocks. His mom told me he had just turned 4 and was a determined little explorer. He had wanted to go outside, but she told him he couldn't. She said she put the top lock across the door before she went to take a quick shower. She wasn't careless. The boy later admitted he used a broomstick to get the lock undone. While his mom was in the shower, she got a phone call from a neighbor that her son had gotten out and was on his bike. She had hoped he was going to his grandparents' house a few doors away. She threw on some clothes and went looking for him. When he wasn't at his grandparents' house, she then guessed correctly about the train tracks. It turns out that the boy set out to go to school so he could be with his big brothers and sisters. Along the way, he got sidetracked.

(Author's note: I did not put on "my journalist's hat" to contact the boy's mother. The family has been through enough as it is. I had no interest in doing my own investigation into the matter. My focus in writing about this is to celebrate Kassandra's heroics and the sparing of a four-year old boy's life.)

The next amazing event of the day was that Katherine wound up making the long drive to school anyway because Kassandra still wanted to go to classes. However, once she got there, Kassandra couldn't stop shaking. "I took Kassandra to her grandparents' house so she could rest in peace and quiet," says Katherine. "She slept for over five hours. Meanwhile, I cleaned like crazy and had a bizarre adrenalin rush for about a month and a half!"

A happy ending wasn't easy for Kassandra. Chief Ken Eborn of the Sunset Police Department hailed her as a hero. Stacey Butler of KSL-TV, Channel 5 in Salt Lake City, and Jason Wood of The Standard-Examiner were two of the reporters who covered the story. Everyone in the community wanted to talk about it. There was even a special assembly at Northridge High.

Kassandra was overwhelmed. She never asked for the limelight even though she clearly earned it. She just wanted to forget the whole thing happened. Outrunning another train might have been easier than getting past her memories of the incident. "I was really, really mad at all those cars who drove by and never stopped. I also remembered there were five cars parked on my side of the tracks that watched the whole thing happen. I was really mad at those people, too. They each had more than one passenger in them, but nobody from those five cars did anything to try to help that boy."

A firefighter friend led Kassandra to the crisis counselor their local department uses. It helped her tremendously. Kassandra is now attending Weber State University. Her longtime dream is to be a hygienist.

I celebrate Kassandra for more than what she did that day. I join her mother in celebrating Kassandra for who she is as a person. "She touches my heart," says Katherine. "I tell her that often. She just has a way about her. In a strange sort of way, what happened at the railroad tracks just seems kind of normal considering it was her."

Now, you too know she is faster than a speeding bullet. Now, you too know she is more powerful than a locomotive. Maybe she is able to leap tall buildings in a single bound. Who knows? If a child in danger is involved, I want Kassandra Guymon!

(Author's note: I'm just wondering aloud here if your wonder took you beyond asking the question of how she was able to run so fast. Did you wonder at all about how in the world Kassandra was able to come to a complete stop after running so fast? She did . . . on railroad tracks no less! Let's be sure to celebrate that, too, and share it as source of belief with a child who thinks he or she cannot do the possible, let alone the impossible!)

Getting Even With Evan

Don't be misled by the title. This is not a story of my seeking revenge. I suppose it is more about seeking answers and just a small piece of peace. This little poem will explain.

In Memory Of
EVAN
"Little King Of The Binky"

I wish I could have watched you walk.

I wish I could have heard you talk.

I wish I could have seen you grow.

I wish you didn't have to go.

Thank you for bringing joy to the world for 363 days.
I miss you.

This is the dedication at the beginning of my first book, *KIDS RULE! The Hopes and Dreams of 21st Century Children.* It's very hard for me to watch people read it. Usually, I have to look away. Sometimes people don't ask me about it, but most times they do.

Evan's story is one worth telling, and since so many have asked me to do so, I decided to save the final celebration in this book for my lost little buddy.

Evan spent his life in a hospital setting. For most of his days, he was a special guest at The Children's Hospital of Philadelphia. This was where we developed our very beautiful bond.

I was serving as a volunteer in the Infant/Toddler unit. In my role, I assisted the nurses by holding sick little ones, changing poopy diapers, doing feedings, getting thrown up on, and anything else that helped the scared children and their families to feel love and comfort. Many times, I did as much of this as Evan would allow.

We connected right away as an odd couple. Our relationship was more than a friendship between an African-American baby boy and a full-grown Irish-American man. We had something of a working relationship. Evan thought he was my boss. I did little to discourage him. After all, I knew the job was temporary.

Physically, Evan had a wide variety of issues, and never got to enjoy real food. There were emotional challenges, too. It is my understanding that he had outside visitors once or twice, but I never met them.

Evan's best friend in the world was his pacifier. He loved pacifiers so much that I nicknamed him, "King of the Binky." If he wasn't snoozing, he was sucking. If he wasn't sucking, he'd be making it crystal clear to you that he absolutely, positively should be! It was really very funny.

The dedicated members of the nursing staff were with him the most, so they made up Evan's next closest friends. Then, there was me. Many people weren't sure how much Evan knew or could see of his surroundings. Never once did I hear baby talk from his lips. Yet, on more than one occasion, I remember certain nurses pleading the case of Evan's abilities to doctors, telling them they would be amazed to see how he reacts when a certain volunteer comes into the room.

I could never seem to put Evan down without him crying. What joy he gave me when we would sit together, him nestled so happily in my arm, with one of his little hands wrapped ever so tightly around my finger. Often, I walked laps around the unit for hours with Evan in one arm, and another little peanut in my other arm. Sometimes, I carried Evan as I pushed one of his neighbors in an infant seat on wheels. No matter what the activity was, the outcome was always the same. Evan wouldn't let me leave until he was sound asleep.

At roughly the halfway point of his short stay in life, Evan threatened to check out early. He went Code Blue and wasn't expected to make it through the night. It just so happened this took place on a night when I was scheduled at the hospital. I felt really sad and helpless being alone with him after being told this was likely Evan's ending.

Nobody seemed to know how, nobody seemed to know why, but Evan managed to hang around. I was quite thankful he survived, but not come Thanksgiving a few months later. I vividly remember spending much of the day with Evan knowing he would never enjoy the taste of turkey or the fun of feasting with family and friends. He was just miserable that day, not only because he was stuck in an oxygen tent, but more importantly because tubes and breathing difficulties meant he couldn't have his binky!

There I was, in his corner, throwing a fit, throwing in the towel on his behalf, praying that the fight be stopped. He was angry and confused because there I was, but I wasn't picking him up to hold him. We were both so frustrated, it's a wonder neither of us ripped that oxygen tent away from him. It all just seemed so unfair.

(The night before the next year's Thanksgiving is when I had a bout of what my grandmother called "The Crying Jacks." I think it was the first time I ever really allowed myself to grieve over the loss of Evan. That sad poem just came out of me.)

On what I knew would be Ev's only Christmas, I knowingly broke hospital rules in buying him presents. (It was one of those rare occasions in which "doing the crime" was worth "doing the time.") I wrapped the gifts but left openings in the paper so there was room to fit his little hands. I felt like every kid should get one chance to open Christmas presents before they get called home.

Together, we unwrapped a couple of really cool, multi-colored additions to the little king's binky collection. I also got him a little snow-white fleece sleeper with footsies and a snowman on the chest. I laughed with the nurses at how adorable his little brown chubby cheeks and body looked in bright white. "He looks like a little angel," someone said.

The next month, Evan died during my regular volunteer shift while I was in Oregon covering a television story about the Kip Kinkel school shootings. In one of the greatest gifts I have ever received, the nurses told me a story of how they dressed Evan in my little white sleeper gift, shortly before he died. They said they thought it was the best way for me to be with him and to help him through his crossing over.

I will remain forever grateful for that priceless gift from the nurses. I felt like I should have been there with Evan. I felt extremely guilty. He obviously disagreed and decided otherwise, choosing instead to retire from here in the role as my boss.

Evan and I were an odd couple. But thanks to some nurses giving such a wonderful closing celebration of his life and my special relationship with him, somehow I now feel even.

Ready Or Not, Here I Go!

Ready or not, here I go. The time has come for this book to end. Getting to this point feels as though I am giving birth to a child myself. It certainly has been a labor of love, lasting more than twice as long as a real pregnancy (but causing many of the same symptoms!)

Like any new parent, I am overwhelmed with emotion. I feel exhausted and excited, and all there is of both. I am beaming with pride over this milestone in my life, while fear tugs on my shirtsleeve and gets in my face. Last but not least, I have hope. I hope this newborn book is well received by the world, and that its positive impact grows every day.

The process of finding and writing about these celebrations of a child has totally consumed me. The book was so important to me that I chose to allow it to take over my life. Though in reality, I never really felt like I had a choice. I simply had to write this book. I just don't know why. I do know it was never work. I always viewed it as answering my life's calling.

Like joyful Jayme Rubright said in the "Diamonds Are A Child's Best Friend" story, *I don't regret a single minute of it. It was the best job I ever had and I didn't even get paid! Yes, it did take up all of my time. Many give up their free time, but we are constantly given something back. I never thought twice about it being a sacrifice.* (At least I was smart enough to copy from a student who got better grades than me!)

Like any other dedicated author, I've spent countless hours in isolation while writing. Notice I didn't say it has "taken" a great deal of my time. That is because I *have* been given so many blessings through writing this book. If time is money, then I am a millionaire in spiritual capital from this process. (If only that paid the bills!)

Through my work on this book, I am more enlightened, encouraged, and even more dedicated to making a difference in the life of a child. I hope in some large or small way, you feel the same having read it.

Relationships with my friends, family, and business associates have been altered, some even damaged while I "lived in a cave" in order to finish this book. Many of my thoughts have been occupied more by the people I've worked with on this book. Oh, what an honor it has been!

I see those written about in this book as "Power People." They have loving, inspirational energy to share. They are cool people doing really cool work. Their celebrations of a child warm hearts and enlighten minds. They serve as symbols of strength, beacons of hope, and roadmaps for lost souls.

How you view the world is strictly your choice, but if do you want to see it in a positive way, I believe I have given you many examples of the pure goodness still alive and well inside human beings. I see others who have helped me greatly with this book in the same light. My own VIP's (very interested people) such as Sharla Feldscher and Steven Druding, have been lifelines to me.

Unbeknownst to me, a hidden beauty of doing this book was that it brought me together with many like-minded people who care about children. These people have been great teachers to me. As I said earlier, we must always have hope. Thanks to them, I now have much more. I hope you do, too.

Little Skylar, who I wrote about, entered the world in fetal distress. Doctors couldn't get her little heart to beat for two and a half minutes on the day of her birth. Today, this miracle baby is lucky enough to be loved and adored by her mother. Today, her joy and happiness are contagious, and she spreads them throughout her school, and her neighborhood. Today, she is "The Beautiful Skye."

Big givers in little bodies like Alison Stoner, Signe Carlson, Felicia Orendorff and Jaclyn Lacey Gyger give me hope. If they are making an impact as young girls, I can only hope I live long enough to learn of the impact they make as adults. Perhaps, they will be part of the next generation to lead the Variety Club to added victories.

I have hope there will be more exceptional children as long as there are educators like Joyce Dunn, Marsha Boehner, Ted Gilbert, Sister Mary Ann Spaetti, Rosemarie Tipton, and "King" David Willauer. I am also comforted knowing there are "Pied Piepers" and people handing out "hugs to go" in working so beautifully to celebrate a child.

I have hope that someday soon I will celebrate the cures for cancer, diabetes, and retinitis pigmentosa with the children in this book. Until then, I feel blessed to have made friends with the families involved.

Judy and Len Hoch lost their precious Colby, but had their lives enriched for five years with his presence. They have also had their lives enriched three more times with their children Katie, Carley, and Kendall.

Penn State continues to give new meaning to the term "higher education." The amazing students who work "for the kids" will surely continue to strengthen the American workforce. I point this out since they are already strengthening the community and the American family.

The Penn State students were right when they said, "Hope surrounds us." It surrounded a four-year old boy on railroad tracks, and it surrounds you and me, too.

Before I go, I must address the covers of this book. To have them showcasing quotes from living legends to me is truly a personal thrill. When people ahead of you in lines for integrity, experience, and credibility, put their reputation on paper for you, they are giving you all they have. Once again, I am extremely grateful.

After a two-hour telephone conversation with Mike Veeck in the final days of writing this book, (and a quick, but healthy dose of talking with Rebecca before she had to go to bed), I became aware of a million and one reasons for the photo that suddenly I knew had to grace the front of this book.

The photo was taken atop the cliffs of Moor. Being an Irish-American, the background is particularly beautiful to me. But, it's what is in the foreground that is breathtaking and spectacular. Little Rebecca Veeck and her parents, Mike and Libby, have touched my heart in ways I cannot explain. While Libby was usually the photographer on journeys with Rebecca, it was Mike who snapped this photo. He says, "I carried her all the way up there, I figured I may as well get the glory for it!"

Being on the book's cover is my surprise gift to Rebecca. I celebrate what vision she has left, and I want her to see herself on the cover of a book *now* in the event she completely loses her eyesight. This is especially important since one of Rebecca's dreams is to write fiction books.

It touches my soul to know I have been a conduit for sharing a million and one ways to celebrate a child. I look forward to the next million and one on my journey. I ask you to keep this book and me in mind if you work with children or charities. Perhaps, it will lead us to share a new celebration.

There's a world filled with children in need of love. I'm just trying to reach as many as I can. Thank you for doing the same.

Thomas Baldrick

thomas@baldrick.com

"This book will have you laughing one minute and crying the next! It offers a unique look at real-life today through the eyes of our children."

—JACK CANFIELD co-author,
Chicken Soup for the Kid's Soul

"Freedom of speech for children! A great book for understanding children and connecting with them on their level!"

—JOHN GRAY, PH.D. author,
Children Are From Heaven

Booking Thomas Baldrick

Website: www.baldrick.com

E-mail: thomas@baldrick.com

School appearances: schools@baldrick.com

Speeches: speeches@baldrick.com

Mailing address: P.O. Box 16216, Philadelphia, PA 19114

Media requests: Sharla Feldscher Public Relations
325 Cherry Street
Philadelphia, PA 19106
215.627.0801
sfeldscher@aol.com